INSIGHT COACHING

From Values to Action

STUART EGLIN

BlueWater Books

INSIGHT COACHING

SOME OF STUART'S PREVIOUS PUBLICATIONS:

the butterfly principle (2009)

The Coaching Four (2011)

It Begins Like This (2015)

Values Count: Believing in what we do (2017)

Blue: Experiments in Sound (2017)

Hang Fire (2019)

FOREWORD

This is the second book in a series of books that I am writing about the underlying themes that have shaped my work over the last few decades, developing a unifying theory to underpin the approaches that I use. I work as a leadership and business coach, and also as a leader in the UK National Health Service. My previous book looked at a values based approach to work. This current book focuses on my coaching practice, describing some of the methods I use and setting them within an insight context. I share some of the techniques that I have applied when working with clients, often co-creating the models and ideas in the moment. My practice is an ongoing development, as with each client I find new ways to work, create new models and ideas. This book sets out where I am with this as it evolves.

Future books will focus on some of the Jungian themes in my working practices: including archetypes in more depth than in this book; and a book on alchemy. I will also describe my approaches to collaboration, creativity and intuition. Over time, this series will build into a comprehensive summary of the broad sweep of my work, taking in the concepts and themes, and setting them within an emerging and overarching framework. Thank you for picking up this book and giving it your time. I hope you find some of the techniques and tools useful.

Stuart Eglin, July 2020
     Liverpool, England.

CONTENTS

OPENING

It had begun as a weird feeling in the pit of my stomach, the sense that it would take just one simple little irritant to push me over the edge so that I would flip and scream at whoever happened to be in front of me at the time. My body was flushed with adrenalin and all of the associated chemicals, as a result of a day when things that I had hoped would work didn't, and I was being blamed for things where I had no influence over the outcome. The chemicals in my body, throwbacks from the animal needs of early mankind, were wanting me to fight, freeze or take flight. In a modern office block, none of those was an option.

This state was something that overwhelmed me at regular points in my life. And I guess it's not just me! Many of us experience burn-out or heavy stress levels as the different aspects of our lives flood over us and leave us feeling out of control.

At different points in my own career, I have looked for support to help with challenges that everyday life throws at us. Sometimes that help came from the boss, or a work colleague who was prepared to listen. Often times it didn't!

In my twenties I figured out that finding a mentor was a good way to find someone with the time, the experience and the integrity to listen and advise without having a vested interest. Then, later in my career I was offered my first opportunity to have some coaching. As often happens, this wasn't exactly coming from a positive space. It was not coaching for me to develop and build my career. No, it was coaching that was offered because the organisation I was working in was being abolished and everyone (above a certain grade!) had access to coaching as part of the transition. This would be an occupational hazard of working in the public sector in the UK. Put positively, this was a generous opportunity to explore my options and avoid unemployment. More sceptically put, it was the employer being seen to be doing something, and looking at ways to minimise redundancy costs. Either way, in my eyes it was a great opportunity to dig myself out of a hole. I took it up enthusiastically and arranged to meet Tony for my first session. Tony was a senior coach for a consultancy based in London. He was offering coaching to a group of us in one-to-one sessions. To maximise efficiency, I met him in a hotel just off a Motorway in the North West of England.

A small meeting room in a modern, with slightly tired decorating, hotel on the outskirts of Warrington. Tony was waiting for me and had a tray with coffee and biscuits on it. This was my first experience of coaching. It was 2002. I had met with mentors before that, but had a niggling feeling that working with someone who is offering "wise counsel" is not exactly empowering. In fact, one of those mentors used to spend most of the hour reflecting on his successes since we had last met. I wasn't sure at times who was supposed to be mentoring who. Other mentors had been incredibly helpful at helping me to network, find new jobs, and solve problems.

Tony brought a very different approach to his sessions with me. He brought questions, not solutions. The answers were left for me to work out. He also challenged a lot of the assumptions I had about the world and the reality that I experienced. Tony was one of five different coaches that I have worked with throughout my career. They have all taken different approaches, but the description I have just given would be one common theme that typifies what coaching is.

Since 2005 I have been working as a coach and developing my own skills. This book sets out the practices that I have developed over the years as they relate to different challenges that arise in the coaching process, and then the second section moves on to look at the insights that arise in the coaching space.

The focus is on finding a coach who can bring objectivity and a questioning challenge to how we work.

© Kate Taylor

There are two big issues in many descriptions of coaching which are worth emphasising. Much of the literature about coaching emphasises that the coach doesn't need to be highly skilled in the work of the client. Coaching practice in leadership and the work-place builds on the early practice in sports coaching. Many people stress that the top class athlete is not trained and coached by someone who is better than them.

Rather, the focus is on finding someone to coach who can bring objectivity and a questioning challenge to how we work. That is the gold dust of coaching. So, we don't necessarily need direct experience to be able to coach someone in their context. Tony had little or no understanding of the world of research management that I was working in. But he did understand career transitions, how to apply skills to a job change, and how to navigate difficult organisational change. That was the space where he was particularly helpful. So, the coach doesn't necessarily bring subject specific exper-tise – in fact sometimes that expertise can get in the way of the coach being objective and challenging the things we take for granted. I have often found myself needing to sit back and avoid leaping in with a solution for a client because I think I understand their situa-tion. I don't! Only they have the detailed knowledge and understanding that will help them to find their own solution.

The second issue, which I often need to stress when I meet a new client, is the need for an eclectic approach. Many coaches identify a specific coaching perspective or training approach and define that as their own particular brand or technique. Thus, if you search for coaches you will find NLP coaches, Behaviourist coaches, Gestalt coaches, Strengths Based coaches. And so on. There are many different approaches. A skilled coach will realise that they need to acquire a diverse mix of approaches and be prepared to draw on them according to the challenges that the client brings to the coaching session. The danger of only having one approach is that the coaching session becomes like the man prowling the house with a hammer – everything begins to look like a nail in need of hammering into the wall. If you try to hammer a screw into the wall, it won't work! We need a toolbox with a tool fit for each occasion, rather than a single tool.

Even more than this, the coach needs to be resourceful enough to work with what presents, start with the intuition that is built from experience, and offer up whatever feels like it fits to the situation. I have called this book "Insight Coaching" because I want to convey the way in which depth coaching can take the coach and the client together to a space of deeper insight and understanding.

PRACTICE

Chapter One

LEADER

I've been a leader at many different levels in organisations now for 30 years. That includes working at junior management, middle management, senior management, director and non-executive. It's true that you don't need direct experience to coach someone in their area of expertise – but it does help if you have context and experience.

The challenges shift and change as we gain experience in leadership. For the client approaching a coach, it may be that this is their first job as a leader or it may be that they have been leading for a while. The challenges brought to coaching change as the perspective matures.

Either way, the challenges that are faced can be played out as a number of key shifts in perspective:

- Managing to Leading
- Player to Manager
- Delegation versus doing
- Emotion and logic
- Typology – everyone isn't like me
- Getting out of my own head
- A values base to work from
- What am I here for?
- Vulnerability – a space to be wrong
- Resilience

Let's take a look at each of these and see what there is to learn in the business of leading.

MANAGING TO LEADING

When we start out as a manager we see the role as technical. Our early steps as a supervisor or manager are all about technical skills of management. We need to learn how to organise tasks, get people to do things for us, and create order in a space of seeming chaos. Then we need to learn the technical aspects of planning and organising. So much to learn, and yet so many of these thing are the job of a manager rather than a leader. What do I mean by this? What is the difference between a manager and a leader? Put simply, a manager is someone holding a title, whose job it is to organise the work of other people or resources – to get things done. A leader may not have any indication of that within their title, and they may not even be senior within their organisation. But they do inspire others to do things – they motivate and encourage, they set or reset a culture within an organisation. This is a much bigger challenge. These two concepts – leadership and management – overlap but they are not the same.

Coaching someone to become a manager is a technical process. It involves talking that person through the things that they need to learn, how to manage processes, how to deal with complexity and uncertainty.

Coaching someone to become a leader is a bigger and more fascinating challenge, where the coach accompanies the person on a journey to excellence and inspiration. On this journey, the coach is exploring with the client, out on a distant journey into the unknown. The coach holds the space for the client to discover who they really are, and what they bring to the world around them.

This is a journey to travel where the client is seeking to be liberated from the restrictions, which they think apply to them. Many of these restrictions are self-imposed. We wrap ourselves in chains within our own heads so much of the time. A coach can help the client to see that many of the assumptions that they make about the reality around them are illusions. We spend so much time "making things up" and trying to read other people's minds, figure out what they are thinking. When we are unsure, we insert our own ideas to fill the gap. So many of these ideas hold us back and restrict our ability to take action.

Many of the assumptions that we make hold us back and restrict our ability to take action.

© *Kate Taylor*

Leadership then is not just about our role in the organisation in which we work, it is also about personal leadership or the way in which we rise to the challenges that we face ourselves. But first we have some aspects of our former self to let go.

PLAYER TO MANAGER

Let's have another look at the role of manager though, as this is where many clients find themselves when they first seek coaching. The transition to management is a tricky one.

Before the client can reach to these heights of personal leadership, she needs to understand some of what she needs to leave behind. It is one of the key challenges faced by the newly promoted leader, turning from player to manager. At the beginning of my own career, fresh from a university degree, I worked for a couple of years as a Community Artist. It was a hugely liberating role in an organisation where I was free with my colleagues to innovate and experiment. Before long, the team leader left to go to train as a Documentary Photographer, and I was asked if I would be the new team leader. It was time to learn the painful transition from player to manager. At first the job seemed easy as I adopted the same style and approach that Dave had used, my predecessor. But that didn't work for very long. I quickly realised that I could no longer be everyone's mate if I wanted to get things done. It was a great opportunity to learn in a really challenging environment. A group of politically active artists were not keen to be managed. I had a lot of new skills to learn. In so many ways this was a great way to learn about management through doing, as the role was so challenging. I had to learn that whilst it is important to distinguish between work and social life, and to realise that we are not meant to be best friends with the people we manage, we will achieve little if we don't earn the respect of those who report to us.

DELEGATION

One of the toughest things we have to learn as a new leader is how to delegate effectively. This is not a short-term problem and it can pervade so many aspects of our life. At the root of this is the feeling that we have mastered a skill and can do it well. It's sometimes easier to do things ourselves rather than waste time explaining it to others. Also, it can be driven by the need to stay in control, to know that things will get done the way we want them to. Beneath these feelings are a couple of issues. Firstly, there is the control issue – delegating well means giving responsibility for something to someone else and ensuring that they have to get it done. It also means making sure that we close off the loop to ensure the task is completed. That can take time, including the need to pass on the skills to do the task. It needs us to realise that time spent in the short-term will save time in the longer term. There may also be feelings of guilt about giving other people work to do, coupled with the feeling that it will make them like us less.

Effective delegation is a key to management success.

© Kate Taylor

All of these interwoven feelings can leave us just getting on with stuff whilst those in our team look on in desperation, looking for meaningful work to do and wondering why we are acting as the bottle-neck to anything getting done.

In coaching, very often the client will arrive into coaching seeking solutions to being overwhelmed, over-work and lack of productivity. Often the first step to a solution can come from looking at how the team around that person are working, to see if the client can delegate more and free themselves up to take a better overview of the work of the team.

To do this, we need to start by looking at some of these underlying feelings and tackling them. The idea that those around us are judging us and unhappy when we pass work to them is an illusion that is best overcome by sitting down with colleagues and handing work to them. The only caveat to this, is that we need to ensure that the work that we delegate is meaningful – that we don't just pass on all the tasks that we don't like. Sure, there are menial tasks in any job, but the share of work in a team needs to done in such a way that everyone gets satisfaction from the work that they do.

Each of us has a preference for working from an emotional or a thinking perspective.

© Kate Taylor

EMOTION AND LOGIC

Leading a team requires us to gain a good under-standing of each of the people who are in the team. If you are familiar with the Myers Briggs Type Indicator, you will know that each of us has a preference for working from an emotional perspective or a thinking perspective – you could see this as heart or head. We are capable of working with both, but one perspective will be stronger for us. The same applies to those that work with us. It is really important to address this pref-erence and work on the other aspect of ourselves. Coaching can really help with this. When talking to a client it is often obvious which their preference is by the language they use – whether they talk about things that they are thinking or things that they are feeling. A thinker will say "I think that we need to…" whereas someone with a feeling preference is more likely to say "It feels to me like this is…"

To develop a breadth of intelligence and percep-tion, we need to be able to work from both of these perspectives. For example, I have worked with many clients who are strongly "thinking" in their preference. They will tend to look at a problem and see the logical solution. They then set out to explain that to the team. Once they have explained it clearly, they will tend to think the job is done. And then, unsurprisingly they become really frustrated when some of the team become resistant and don't understand why the change is taking place and why their "feelings" haven't been taken into account.

So, we need to build an understanding that both heart and mind need to be addressed if we are working to persuade people who work with us. Explaining the logic and argument is only a part of the challenge. We then need to address how people are feeling about this, and make sure that they are heard.

TYPOLOGY – EVERYONE ISN'T LIKE ME

Are you familiar with typology? Have you carried out the Myers-Briggs Type Indicator test? Many people have – if you haven't it might be a useful test to complete and have feedback on. It's a test developed in the 1940s and 1950s by mother and daughter Katharine Cook Briggs and Isabel Briggs Myers. It is based on the work of Carl Jung, looking at typology in personality, which he wrote about in "Personality Types". Jung put forward the theory that we are made up of various types or characteristics and that the particular combination of types we favour will determine our preference for behaving in situations. The four pairs of types that were developed for the Myers-Briggs Type Indicator are Introversion / Extroversion, Sensing / Intuiting, Thinking / Feeling, Perceiving / Judging. There is not room to go into detail about this test here, but I mention it because aspects of this test and the preferences of people are really useful to understand as it helps us to be more effective in how we communicate with others. Let me explain.

If your typology gives you a preference for thinking rather than feeling, you will tend to look at things from a logical perspective rather than an emotional one.

Another way of describing this would be head and heart. An example of this would be someone who wants to change job roles of the staff within the department which they run. They know what they want to do, and they have **thought** it through, preparing clear arguments for why this is the best approach. When they take this to the team to discuss, they come away from the conversation incredibly confused because some members of the team seem to understand the arguments but are still opposed and keep saying that no-one is listening to how they **feel** about it. There are clues in the use of language. For the person with a thinking preference, it doesn't come naturally to work through the feelings of those for whom this is a preference. This whole situation can easily become fraught with conflict.

Part of the way to the solution here is to realise that these are not fixed attributes that we work from. They are preferences. So, we may have a very strong preference for "feeling" but that is not absolute. We are still perfectly capable of applying a "thinking" perspective to things. It just doesn't come that easily. If we find that we are not getting things done the way we want them, it is worth looking at whether we are over-emphasising one particular trait and not addressing the fact that others in the team may be very different from us in how they see things.

The cliché that talks about making sure that we take "hearts and minds with us" as we proceed is very much about this issue. It is important to consider how we are putting things across, what tactics we are applying to ensure that we take the team with us. This doesn't just apply to the first pair of types. It also applies to the others. We will have a preferred typology – knowing that typology is like having the keys to the vault, understanding how we differ from others and being mindful of that is like understanding what is in the vault.

It is a key part of the coaching process to draw out the client to understand different perspectives; to realise that there is not just one right way to look at things. Insight comes through looking at things from the perspective of people who are very different from us. If this is difficult to achieve in dialogue, it can sometimes help to have a third chair in the room. Place an imaginary "other person" in the third chair and ask the client to imagine how that person would be reacting to the situation that is being discussed. Then, once they have given time to that, ask them to actually sit in the chair and be that person for a while to see if that changes the perspective even more clearly. This simple exercise can create massive "aha" moments, realisations that are otherwise not open to us.

GETTING OUT OF MY OWN HEAD

For so many of us, myself included, it is all too easy to spend our lives in our thoughts. Drifting along. Have you ever walked or driven somewhere along a familiar route and on arrival been unable to recollect any details of the route? That tends to happen when we are in our heads, lost in thoughts. A part of the brain where automatic processing can happen is taking care of things like walking or driving the car, whilst we process a mish-mash of ideas, thoughts and concepts. There is nothing wrong with this – as long as you are driving safely! In fact, walking and thinking can be a great way to problem solve. But it can be problematic if we are truly in the moment. It doesn't serve us as a way of being in the world when we are sitting listening to someone, but not really hearing them because we are too busy listening to our thoughts.

We often talk about needing to get out of our head, the need to shift from thinking in abstract to engaging properly with the world around us. In earlier sections of this chapter I was drawing attention to the difference between thinking and feeling. However, there is another aspect to this that we also need to consider. Metaphorically we are talking about connecting with head and heart, there is also the instinctive thinking, sometimes referred to as a gut feeling. That expression draws us to the stomach.

Whether you want to see this as metaphorical or symbolic – what I am wanting to look at is the role of head, heart and gut in the way that we present to the world, and make decisions. It's too simplistic to just see a decision as being a balance between head and heart. There is also a role for our instinctive thinking, which resides in the stomach.

Recent research is showing some evidence for us having minds in the heart and the stomach. When we experience 'butterflies' in our stomach this is an example of what researchers are suggesting is the connection via nerves that makes it possible for the mind / minds to function in different parts of our body.

This is why we really do need to balance out the

way we look at the world. Just analysing the world with the mind that is in the head, gives us a partial view of things.

Let me give you a practical example. When a client wants help with a difficult decision where there is no simple right answer − maybe they want to decide whether to take a job offer or stay where they are − there are steps we can take as a coach to help them unpack the issue and look at the pros and cons. But sometimes this still doesn't get the client to the solution. This is a good time to look at the issue from these three perspectives. We get into this space by asking:

- What do you **think** is the right thing to do?
- How do you **feel** about this decision, what does your heart tell you?
- What do you **instinctively** want to do?

Each of these brings us into a different way of considering the question. Once we have sat with each of these for a few minutes, the decision may be easier to make.

A VALUES BASE TO WORK FROM

In 'Values Count' (my previous book) I wrote about values based working. That book looked at why working from values is so important. In this book, I want to take those ideas further, and look at how values can be applied in action through an effective coaching process, so that we open up our thinking, become aware of our potential and truly realise it. These values are as relevant to the Leader in their work as they are to the coach in their practice.

The coaching process itself also needs to be strongly based in values. In this section I set out a suggested value-set based on The Six Perfections or Six Paramitas.

1. **Generosity** – when we bring this attribute into our practice as a leader and as a coach, we shift the focus. Instead of looking at any situation that presents and thinking 'what can I get out of this situation' or 'what's in it for me', we look instead at what we have to offer. Generosity can relate to money, but not only to money – it can refer to giving our attention or time to something or someone. It can also relate to giving guidance and support. As a coach, we are not there to impose our own thoughts and ideas on the client. We should enter the coaching process with an emptiness, ready for what the client brings – generous with our ideas, but gentle with them too.

2. **Ethics** – we have a responsibility to practice leadership and coaching ethically. Both professions require high standards of morality to be practiced. When we practice with regard to ethics, we will deliver our work to the highest standard. The failings of

leadership in recent years all too often stems from poor morality, a lack of regard for others.

3. **Patience** – this attribute refers to the ability to look at situations and consider them in a calm and reflective way, to avoid anger and to work hard to understand the other person's situation and feelings. The end point may still be that we push through a decision that we know is right, but the application of patience makes sure that we carry people with us.

4. **Joyous Effort** – if we apply ourselves joyously to the work that we do and apply a mind of curiosity to our work, we will find easier routes to solutions. Applying a mind of joyous effort, with an eye on the end point, the underlying purpose of what we are working for, will ensure that we approach our work more lightly. This will have a profound effect on our productivity and effectiveness.

5. **Concentration** – in this 'always on, always connected' world it is so easy to flit from distraction to distraction. We should instead aim for focus and concentration. Developing the ability to apply single-minded concentration as a leader will make us so much more effective. For the coaching process, it is also critical to apply concentration to the client, being fully there throughout the session.

6. **Wisdom** – this attribute combines with the act of generosity. We should ensure that we are constantly learning. A leader who doesn't read and study about leadership, is a poor leader. A coach who doesn't continue to study and learn about coaching is a poor coach. We acquire knowledge and technique so that we can share it with others. Through greater wisdom, that comes from study, we become better at what we do. It is not just the acquiring of knowledge, but also what we do with it that generates wisdom. We work at various levels to gain insight and deeper wisdom so that we are able to see beyond the surface, beyond the obvious. We then develop the ability to understand unhelpful thinking patterns, emotional triggers and to understand the realities of complex systems.

This framework gives us a basis from which to work. Using the six perfections and reflecting on them regularly will ensure that we can apply what we do in the most effective way.

WHAT AM I HERE FOR?

There is a quote, often attributed to Mark Twain, although apparently he didn't say it. It goes:

. . .

"The two most important days in your life are the day you are born and the day you find out why."

Twain or not, it's a line worth thinking through and devoting some time to. Do you meditate? If you don't that's a skill you could do with learning. An effective meditation can be just a few minutes of time spent in quiet contemplation. My morning practice includes a daily seven minute meditation. Sometimes the meditation focuses on stilling the mind, other times it is used to think about a particular issue. The issue "what am I here for?" could be something that you spend time on.

If you don't know the "why" of your daily work, how can you decide what to focus on? Many clients who I work with are not really sure what they want to do with their working lives. That is not unusual at all. It's common to not be clear about a career path, or about the sort of work we want to do. But that is not the same as being clear about the contribution you want to make. Again, this is about what we give into living, rather than what we take out.

A good starting point for this is to spend some time working out what you **don't** want to do. Being clear on that can avoid a lot of false starts. Sometimes we work this out by trial and error. I have had jobs in the past that were great to begin with, but as I gained experience and mastery of the job, I realised that this was really not something that I wanted to do long term. It didn't play to my strengths, attributes or interests. Working that out is really important.

Spending time thinking about why we are here, so

that we can be clearer about our contribution is helpful. But often the solution doesn't just drop into our minds in a moment of revelation. The answer comes from applying the values base I described in the last section. If we are engaged in meaningful work that fires us up, and makes us want to get out of bed, we can be sure that we are on the right path to figuring out the answer to the deeper question, why am I here. So, it's not a quick solution, and sometimes we come across it almost by accident, but once we have found the answer we will work from a place of inner passion, alive to the work that we are doing.

For me, the process took a long time. I had worked with colleagues who brought this passion to their work. I would look at them and wish that I had their passion for what I did. After working on various projects, looking for the things that I wanted to do, finding ways of working that I thought were making a real difference in people's lives – I realised almost by accident that I was now working from that place of passion. I would find myself talking about my work to people, and feel a surge of energy from within as I became more animated about the work. I had found it!

VULNERABILITY – A SPACE TO BE WRONG

There is so much talk of the need for businesses to take risks. I have worked in the English National Health Service for most of my career where there has been a quest for greater innovation for years. But innovation doesn't happen in a severely risk averse culture. Of course we don't want risks that mean that someone is going to die or get injured. But if we don't create a culture (and we do influence culture as leaders) that is receptive to risk and failure, then we won't learn or innovate.

We need to create a space to be wrong. This, like so often where we are looking for behaviours, is not achieved by telling people they can take risks and get things wrong. It only happens when we model the behaviour ourselves. In leadership, we need to be able to get things wrong because we are experimenting, and be prepared to admit that we got it wrong. Oh, and apologies are good too. It's the same as with children, people don't model their behaviour based on what we tell them, they model it on what we actually do.

We need to show how to take risks – within parameters that are safe – and have in place review processes so that we know when something is going wrong and can stop it.

Vulnerability is about being a leader who can open your feelings up in a calm way. Sometimes it helps if the leader admits that they are fearful for the future too – that shows humanity. Teams can see through false optimism. They can read when the leader is being positive without authenticity.

A team that has an open and honest relationship where it is ok to admit our fears, and to be vulnerable in the safe space with colleagues, will perform higher and achieve greater results.

When we are a new leader we can get caught up in the myth of the hero leader who has no vulnerable side. That is the route to burn-out. The better path to follow is one where we own our vulnerability, have a plan, and admit that there is always uncertainty.

So just to be clear, I am not suggesting that the leader relinquishes all responsibility by getting in touch with their feelings and opening up to all the worries there are. That's not it at all – but there are times when it is helpful to open up and share our vulnerability, as long as it is accompanied with honesty and a continuing sense of direction for the team as a whole.

RESILIENCE

It has become a 'buzz' word, resilience. It means different things in different settings. At the extreme it is about finding ways to survive increasingly stressful work environments. Let's look at some definitions:

Resilience:
1. the capacity to recover quickly from difficulties; toughness.
2. the ability of a substance or object to spring back into shape; elasticity.

Wouldn't it be great if we had the elasticity to spring back into shape after a particularly challenging day? Without the aid of a glass of wine?

Some days at work can be more challenging than others.

© Kate Taylor

In leadership, whilst it is really important to be able to show the vulnerability that I described in the last section, it is also critical to display resilience. Teams look to their leader to show optimism, and a healthy balance of realism and idealism. This isn't something that sits within our genes, we can teach ourselves to shift perspective. Instead of looking for the challenges and problems around us, we can instead focus on how to improve things. Appreciation of what we have is a good place to start. Even in dire circumstances, it is possible to look for good things.

This can begin with an exercise that is used to reduce the danger of catastrophisation – the tendency to imagine that awful things are going to happen. If a client is facing possible redundancy, instead of starting by focusing on the positive, which would rightly be seen as potentially deluded, it might make more sense to start with 'worst case scenario'. Get the client to focus on the worst thing that could **realistically** happen. For most clients this won't be as bad as their catastrophising was leading them to believe. If they begin by suggesting they could lose their home, their family, their sanity etc. – ask them to check in with what is realistically going to happen. Setting out the realistic worst case is hugely empowering. It serves as a starting point that we then 'ladder' away from by looking at a series of other opportunities. We create a set of options, some of them within the client's control that helps to build resilience.

I will look in more detail in chapter three at some of the approaches that can be used to overcome this loneliness in senior positions, which also help to build resilience.

It's also really helpful to address the inner driving force within each of us. We may be critical of colleagues, but that is often nothing to the criticism that we save for ourselves. In the coaching process, it is important to create a safe space for the client where they can explore this driving inner critic and look at ways to nurture and support the self. How can this be done? The coach needs to 'call out' the inner critic when that voice is apparent. As the client reveals this tendency to self-criticise – usually with lots of "I should haves" that is where the coach can challenge. Pushing back with "aren't you being a bit harsh on yourself" may work. If that doesn't work, it may be necessary to shift perspective, by asking the client what they would think if this was a colleague, would they be so harsh? Be specific, name the colleague – very rarely are we as harsh to colleagues as we are to ourselves.

Very rarely are we as harsh to colleagues as we are to ourselves.

© Kate Taylor

Chapter Two

ENTREPRENEUR

It is very unusual these days to be working in an environment that doesn't require entrepreneurial skills. The days when we worked for a large organization which paid us in return for our labour, and we just did what was in our job description, seem long in the past now for so many of us. The economy has changed so much since the economic crash of 2008, and also in response to new tech and digital solutions. Many people now either work for themselves, or work in small organisations. Those that work in larger organisations often find themselves needing to run smaller units within the larger organisation as if they were in some kind of market environment. Leaving aside the political perspective of this, and whether it leads to better outcomes, the reality is that for many of us, entrepreneurial skills are key. We need to have an entrepreneurial mindset in order not just to survive, but to thrive.

PUBLIC SECTOR VALUES

My career began working for a charity. We ran services for disabled people. Part of the responsibility of leadership was to raise funds to enable us to deliver the work. This wasn't a charity with invested funds that paid the bills! We had to raise all of our funds to deliver the work that we wanted to do. An entrepreneurial spirit was the key to success. Any idea needed to be appealing to someone who was prepared to fund it. The end user of the service wasn't necessarily paying for it, but someone had to provide the funds in order for us to deliver the service.

After seven years in a charity, I moved to the English Health Service. In recent years, this too has taken on a market approach, and in the last six years my work has required us to 'income generate' to function. Working as a social entrepreneur means making sure that the ideas we develop serve the agenda of one of the agencies we work with so that we can attract funding.

Public sector values do differentiate what we do from the work of a commercial entrepreneur, although probably less than might be imagined. Our focus is on covering our costs, and perhaps generating enough of a surplus for us to be able to develop new ideas for future funding. There is not the profit element as a driver, but we still need to balance the books.

This mind-set, looking at the work that we do from an entrepreneur's perspective can radically change the way we see work. It opens up the opportunity to be innovative. If all we see is the funds we have allocated at the start of the financial year, we are limited to what we can provide within that budget. If instead of that, we follow a very different approach, where we look at:

- What are we aiming to achieve, and what are some of the novel ideas that we could apply to that aim?
- How could we deliver this within a framework of public sector values?
- Who would be prepared to invest funds in these ideas?

It's a different mind-set completely. It frees us up to think more creatively about the work that we do.

As I have said earlier in the book, we often impose constraints on ourselves, convincing ourselves that they are external, when they are not. We convince ourselves that a course of action is not possible because the organisation won't allow it, or our boss won't agree, or there must be a law that stops me doing that. If we look closely at this, often none of those is true, and the only person stopping us from acting is ourselves.

Once this is clear, we can move forwards, free up the work that we do – and enable ourselves to do things that make our work more exciting and innovative. The first step will get us on the path to something transformational. This isn't a rehearsal for another life – this is it, a precious human life, act as though it is the real thing.

HOW I BECAME AN ENTREPRENEUR

I have already mentioned that I spent 7 years working for a charity and then have been working in the NHS since 1989, nearly 3 decades. And yet, here I am calling myself a social entrepreneur. How come?

The charity I worked for in the 1980s was a regional charity which grew very rapidly, delivering services to people in need. Throughout its growth, there was a vision and overall direction set by a Chief Executive who had come from a commercial background. He really understood how to encourage young people to innovate and experiment. We could take an idea from that morning and be working on it later the same day. He really did instil in us the sense that anything was possible. This was, I think, the roots of my entrepreneurial spirit. It encouraged me to bring new ideas into the workplace and play with them. The first team I worked in, and soon became the leader of was a team of Community Artists. By definition there was plenty of creativity around – but the creativity reached beyond the work itself and into the ways in which we worked too.

Our Chief Executive would regularly bring philan-thropists and business people into our space to meet us so that we could talk about the work that we did. Making a pitch didn't come naturally to me. Like many coaching clients with whom I work, I wouldn't describe myself as a natural seller of things. But that is a myth that we often get caught up in. The idea that selling is a particular skill (like networking) that we are either born with or don't have at all, is simply not true. In the last chapter we talked about typology and particular traits that make some things easier for us to do than others. Clearly, a particular typology will find it easier to pitch ideas because their strengths lend themselves to being able to do that. But if you ask a highly introverted individual to talk about something that they have a strong belief in and are highly committed to, they will show a remarkably persuasive ability to pitch for it.

So, the degree of commitment to something makes it easier to show the entrepreneurial ability to pitch something. When I worked for the charity, we were providing services that improved the lives of disabled people. It was easy to pitch for this, to speak with real conviction about what we were doing. This was then the first step in my journey to understanding what it means to be an entrepreneur.

These experiences early in my career helped me to understand the importance of feeling empowered, able to grasp the initiative. I know that empowerment and passion are two words that are massively over-used and abused these days. But, as I explained in the previous section, we often have more control over things that are going on around us than we assume that we do.

In coaching, we are working with the client to reveal some of these limitations, and create the ability to take control of aspects of our career and life, and realign them to fit what our aspirations are.

To gain real insight with the client, requires digging deep into assumptions. We need to work together to look at all those situations where we dive into "binary thinking" for example. We are presented with a choice of two options – and that leads into a forced decision, when there may have been other choices we could have taken. Always be wary of the "yes / no" choice or the "this or that" choice. Being given decisions to make like this will drive us in a particular direction.

Our manager could for example, ask us whether we are happy to take on a major new piece of work. This feels like a yes or no decision – I can do it (manager is happy) or no I can't do it (manager is unhappy). Add in the thoughts that are in brackets in the previous sentence and we are pushed into just the one option. Go back two steps, and look at all of the options – for example, we could do a bit of the work that is required and suggest a colleague to work with us on the rest of it, or we could suggest that we do the work, but not for at least a month, or we do it in return for dropping something else. If we worked on this scenario for a while we would probably see lots of possible options.

Being forced, or forcing ourselves into the binary choice is really unhelpful if we want to create choices and feel more in control.

A bit of lateral thinking can often create opportunities that may not at first be apparent. The work of Edward de Bono is particularly useful for getting us to think differently about scenarios. His work on lateral thinking, six thinking hats and many other techniques taught me to open up my thinking and behave much more as an entrepreneur would, never taking things for granted or accepting the evidence in front of us.

PUBLIC SECTOR ENTREPRENEURS

There is nothing new about the idea of being entrepreneurial in the public not-for-profit sector. Many elements of current public sector provision emerged from highly innovative and entrepreneurial ventures in the past, often the idea of an inspired individual seeking a solution to a problem.

Interesting examples of organisations that have supported public sector focused entrepreneurial activity include the work of Ashoka, which was created in 1978. Its founder Bill Drayton looked for four qualities – creativity, entrepreneurial quality, social impact of the idea, and what he called ethical fibre. In 1998, NESTA was formed in the UK under the Blair / Brown government, using funds from the National Lottery to establish a fund that would encourage social entrepreneurship and innovation in response to public sector challenges.

More recently online initiatives like crowd funding and micro-lending have also had an impact, breaking down the traditional models of funding and the bureaucratically driven approach to public sector provision.

The four qualities set out by Ashoka are interesting because they emphasise the importance of social impact and ethical fibre. This brings us back to the fundamental need for an underpinning ethical base to entrepreneurship in the public sector.

Working in this way can be hugely challenging. The process of insight coaching, working from a values base to create a focused approach to the work, can provide a framework to clarify the purpose and the work that flows from that.

Recent initiatives in coaching, especially in the public sector have generated a performance culture in coaching, looking for indicators of success, and narrowing down the coaching process so that it can be measured. This is really unhelpful. An insight coaching approach aims for transformation, rather than transaction. Working outwards from the client, rather than starting with the organisational imperative, creates a different coaching relationship. If the performance management culture continues to invade the coaching space, it will lead to a reduction in the effectiveness of coaching. We need to be focusing on what matters, rather than just focusing on what we can count.

As coaching in this social entrepreneurial space works at the intersection between "social value" and "entrepreneurial focus", it is really important that we enable the individual to drive the coaching approach. Starting with where the client is, driving through their value-base and getting crystal clear about the end point – that is the start of the coaching contract.

We will not achieve wider engagement with an innovative and entrepreneurial culture if we micromanage the process and performance manage the outputs.

To truly create innovative cultures, we need to encourage play and experimentation. I will talk in a later chapter about the importance of creativity in coaching itself and also in the workplace. As well as creativity, the essence of play is the way that it opens us up to possibilities.

Watch the playground in break time at a secondary school – eleven to eighteen year olds. Even though the older students are heading into young adulthood, they still know how to play and relax. We so often lose that playfulness in adulthood. Ask a group of adults to do an "ice breaker" and many of them will groan and look embarrassed at the idea. But it is in playful mode that we open ourselves to discovery.

The entrepreneurial approach will emerge from a work environment which has play and creativity built into it.

MARKET SENSIBILITIES

Thanks to the onslaught of neoliberalism in the world, we all find ourselves working in the context of the market. Competition exists even when we are working with people who we see as collaborators. It would be naïve to ignore the workings of the market whatever the context in which we are working.

Many years ago, as the internal market was introduced into the NHS, I began to explore ideas around the interface between competition and collaboration or co-operation. Coining the word "co-opetition" – not my invention of course, it goes back almost a hundred years – I began to look at how people and organisations can operate at the interface between competition and co-operation. In most sectors there are laws determining the extent to which co-operation can happen without collusion (which would be illegal!)

I have already emphasised the role of coaching in creating different options, and of resilience. These come together in a deeper understanding of the market in which we operate. The coach can open up the client's thinking to encourage a greater flexibility, seeking solutions that are win / win rather than win / lose. Combine this Stephen Covey principle with the Edward de Bono's principle that the first solution we find may not be the best one – and you can develop an approach to problem solving that is more sophisticated and generates better outcomes.

Having a greater understanding of the market in which we are functioning, and spending time researching the needs of the other players in the market can help us to think of novel approaches that combine the strengths of many of the players, rather than just playing a zero sum game where either I win or you do. One way to achieve this would be through repeated questioning – not settling for the first answer to any situation. Instead, ask "why" repeated times until we get to a richer understanding.

VALUE PROPOSITIONS – BEYOND FINANCES

In this space of public entrepreneurship, it is really important to measure what we are doing in a diverse range of ways, not just with the bottom line of finances. A fabulous book by Alexander Osterwalder called "Business Model Generation: a handbook for visionaries, game changers, and challengers" is a really useful resource. The book focuses on how to take value propositions and turn them into meaningful ways to determine how well we are doing. We do need to balance the books, but this is not a good way of looking at what we are trying to achieve ultimately. Whether we look at our own personal role, or the wider perspective of the organisation we are in, we need to clarify what the deeper purpose of our work actually is. When we have identified this deeper purpose, we can then start to unpack what that looks like. What does success look like? How can we identify it? Is there a clear way to measure it? If not, do we need a proxy that we can measure? If we can't measure it at all, what is it useful to look at? For example, if the core purpose of a programme of work, is to support career development, what does success look like? The salary is not the only measure here – we also need to look at job satisfaction and what the person is achieving with the work that they do.

We tend to steer away from things that are not easy to measure, but it is worth the effort and attention to unpack this. In any area, with a bit of thought, we can identify what to look at, and how to capture it.

This is every bit as relevant to the coaching process itself, as it is to the outcome for the client.

WHAT DOES THIS ALL MEAN FOR THE CLIENT?

To survive the modern world of work, the digitally connected space where many of us work, the knowledge economy – we need to equip ourselves with the skills of the entrepreneur. Earlier in this chapter I explained how this is increasingly relevant to more of us as organisations adopt entrepreneurial techniques. But this is not just restricted to the organisation. Individuals need to take on entrepreneurial techniques too.

It is now a while since Tom Peters spoke about the concept of "Brand You", but it has not lost any of its currency. In the world where organisations are becoming both larger, global and dominant, whilst also being smaller and leaner – survival comes easier to those who see themselves as their own brand irrespective of who they work for. This does not mean that we should be subversive or undermine the organisations that we work for. That is not the point I am making. Rather, we need to see ourselves as a brand would. This means that we need to be clear what we stand for, what we bring to the world, and what it is that we need to preserve. Trust takes a long time to build, but seconds to destroy.

To gain insight into how we work, we need to figure out more than just our curriculum vitae . That document acts as an historical document of our roles for many people but not of our values and the beliefs that drive us. Beyond the jobs and responsibilities, it is important to identify the specific things that we have achieved, and also the skills or attributes that we have. If we can also make sure that we show how they are transferable, that is a great advantage. This starts to build our "Brand" and will enable us to see ourselves as an entrepreneur in our own career.

This can be especially useful in showing the coaching client that the obvious route to a new job – looking at job adverts - is like trying to win the lottery. Instead, we need to look laterally and diversely for the next work opportunity. Networking is a key step. If we have done the work to identify our defining characteristics within our brand, we will have done what we need to do to open the conversation out so that we are exploring new opportunities with those with whom we network, rather than just existing jobs. The best job after all, is the one that we design with someone so that it becomes uniquely fitted to us. If we can do that, we can work with the company or organisation as though we are a sub-contractor or independent, even if we are on the payroll. It is a key shift in thinking that is enormously empowering.

Coaching, as it achieves insight, becomes about empowering the client. It becomes a process of opening up the client to new ways of thinking, to realising that many of the restrictions that we think we have, are illusions in our head. They are the stories that we tell ourselves. Until we let these illusions go, we cannot be truly free to find our best selves.

By letting go of the restrictions in our own heads, we can be free to find our best selves.

© Kate Taylor

Chapter Three

ISOLATION

It can be a real challenge working as "the boss". Coaching can be a great space in which to talk safely about the isolation of being in a leadership position. In any working environment, there will be times when we need to explore difficult issues with someone who is not involved. We can talk to colleagues, we can talk to family and friends – but ultimately it's lonely at the top. The difference with a coach is that they don't bring their own agenda to the issues that face us.

In this section we will look at some of the issues that are thrown up by the solitary nature of being a leader.

IMPOSTER SYNDROME

One thing that has struck me as remarkable is the extent to which feelings like that of not fitting in, are so universal. We can find ourselves feeling like the imposter and wonder whether anyone else feels the same way. When these feelings are happening to us, we manage to convince ourselves that we are the only person who feels like that. This is not the case – many people experience imposter syndrome. It manifests as the opposite of having a sense of entitlement.

Here's a couple of examples.

It was a business dinner. Senior leaders from across the region had been invited. One of them was standing next to me at the pre-dinner drinks, chatting intently. Then he lowered his voice, "I'm not good at this whole schmoozing thing, Stuart. It makes me feel very out of my depth and uncomfortable." This was someone who I had seen acting gregariously at meetings, full of humour, and in a very senior role. He ran an entire division within his organisation, and always had a witty response when in conversation. On the outside he always appeared so confident, and yet here he was admitting that inside he felt out of place, uncomfortable. Here we were in an evening social venue and he was feeling really ill at ease.

Then a few weeks later I was coaching a Chief Executive of an organisation. She too was talking about the immense feeling of unease she had when she was at meetings with peers. She felt out of her depth. There was the overwhelming feeling that someone would open the door, walk in and tap her on the shoulder. "You shouldn't be in this room. Come on, time to leave". She actually expressed it to me in that way, that she was not meant to be there, and would be found out!

We all worry at times that someone is going to challenge us. This is especially true when we are in a situation where we are learning new skills. In order to grow through learning we will inevitably move out of our comfort zone. What has struck me from coaching a large number of clients is just how common imposter syndrome is, that feeling that we shouldn't be in the space, in role, in the situation. The worry that someone will "call us" on it, and reveal us as a bit of a fraud.

Now, I am sure there are some people out there who are remarkably self-assured. They had a solid upbringing with incredibly encouraging parents, they went to schools that encouraged them to be confident, and they have only had experiences which confirm that they are brilliant. But most people aren't like that.

We have had experiences at home, at school and at work where someone has told us we are stupid, or useless, or out of our depth. We seem to internalise that and it becomes the inner critic. It's our own inner critic that creates this feeling that we are an imposter.

The empowering thing from those two opening stories I have set out is that often the most unlikely person is battling with imposter syndrome. And of course, because we can't read people's minds, we don't know who is struggling with it.

So, the next time you are sitting in a meeting feeling slightly queasy and worried that someone is going to tap you on the shoulder, just look around the room. The chances are that at least one other person in the room has the same feeling as you. And doesn't that make you feel better? And just maybe that makes the syndrome evaporate!

It's the first step of course, but in seeing the problem and then realising that we are not the only one, we begin to tackle the issue.

The next step in dealing with the issue, comes through a better understanding of the difference between how we feel on the inside and how we look to others. This is linked to an awareness that others are experiencing the same feelings. We very rarely display externally what is going on in our inner world. Grasping this, it becomes possible to ease the feelings within, as we realise that our sense of being an imposter is just a thought. Nothing more. Detaching ourselves from the thoughts that we are having is an important skill to learn. Through doing this we become able to better control what is going on. This sounds harder than it is!

I mentioned above that there is a strong link between imposter syndrome and the inner critic. It is this inner critic, driven by the base fears that drives flight or fight, which kicks in when we feel like the imposter. The inner critic thinks it is trying to protect us. Instead of resisting it, fighting it – we are better to invite it in. Say hello and acknowledge it. And then, as we do with those imposter feelings, see it as just a voice, not a voice of truth, but a voice that we create with the best of intentions. If we listen to it and obey it, we will never be as great as we can be, we will stop ourselves from doing things that we haven't done before, from doing something that we don't know how to do yet.

As you can see, this whole reaction pattern will be at its strongest when we are trying something new, or when we are promoted into a new role. We chastise ourselves for being stupid, for not knowing how to do what is needed, for not having the required knowledge. We need to see that this is not logical – of course we don't know how to do this, it's new! That's the point! This is how we learn and grow.

Overcoming imposter syndrome, and its agent the inner critic, is the key to progress. Coaching can support the client through this and help with gaining an insight into what is going on inside the client, and how to shift into a new way of looking at things.

DETACHMENT

The coach and the client both share the need to understand and implement detachment. This will help to make the coach more effective, and if the coach can also pass on this skill to the client it will help them to function more effectively as a leader. Let us look in more detail at what is meant by the word 'detachment'.

At first, it seems that we are describing something that is the opposite of attachment. Thus, it would mean that we need to find a way to be removed from, or distant from the client. But that is not what we mean by detachment. Detachment is a combination of two key attributes – compassion with objectivity. In working with the client (and also in working as a leader) we need to enter into the situation or problem that presents to us and show compassion, get an understanding of what the other person is feeling, identify with it. But this does not mean that we identify with the feelings so much that we lose ourselves in them, totally identify with them and go with our heart. We need the objectivity that partners with compassion to ensure that we hold back – this is detachment. It's at the counterpoise of connection without identification.

This is achieved by applying two sets of skills. The first set we bring is the application of logic to the situation. This entails checking the facts, whilst placing to one side the emotions in the situation (not discarding or rejecting the emotions as they are important). What can we actually determine is happening in this situation? Doing this whilst showing compassion enables us to be of optimal help to the other person. The second set of skills derives from the value set or ethics that we bring to the situation. Bringing a clear set of values to the table enables us to navigate through the problem and gain insight into what is going on. The combination of logic and values brings a compass to our approach and enables us to see through the confusing details of a situation (the obscurations), so that we can look with clarity at what is going on.

Now, we are in a position to work with the other person, through the questions that we ask to support them as they achieve a shift in perspective. It is not the job of coaching to give the client answers, it is about providing key questions that bring the client to the answers themselves, with true ownership of the answers. This holds true for the leader as well as with those that they lead too.

Detachment is this ability to hold the situation, be nurturing and supportive whilst at the same time having the objectivity and moral compass to be of help in the situation. It is the exact opposite of the person who dives in with solutions and suggestions, "I'll tell you what I'd do in that situation". As a coach, and often as a leader, it is the hardest thing to do, to resist the temptation to dive in with a solution (it's your solution if you do, not theirs!) To metaphorically sit on our hands is what we have to do, acknowledge that the solution is in your head, let it go and wait. Instead of coming up with a solution, think of a skilful question to ask. How about "What is really going on here?" This creates a space where the other person can really look at the situation and see whether they have missed anything. It also gives them the chance to see things outside of their own world.

When we use detachment in this way, we are able to really support the other person. In this section I have emphasised the importance of this skill, whilst showing that the attribute of detachment is a key element of the approach of the coach as well as the leader.

BUILDING A COMMUNITY

The coach, working with a leader, can address the isolation of the role by looking broadly at community. As a leader we will have a responsibility for developing the community of those who report to us. But, as I have described above, detachment is an essential skill, but one that will lead to being separate from the communities that we build. The leader needs to form their own community for support. With this in mind, networking is a key skill. In my experience of coaching, many people balk at the idea of networking. "I'm not a good networker", is a regular opening response. But few of us are, until we build the skill. And when we think of networking, we often are drawn to the "selling" world of formal networking events, where no-one gets a sale because everyone is selling. This is not the sort of networking that I am referring to. Building a network is a skill that comes from a vivid curiosity about other people. It's not about telling others what we do (that comes in time, of course) – the starting point is an interest in the other person. Through this approach we can build a strong community around us of people who we can build trust with, and share ideas and challenges.

For my own network, I have built trusted connections with people from a wide variety of backgrounds. This has helped me to learn a lot about so many different sectors, and glean ideas that can be adapted to my own workspace.

COACHING, MENTORING AND PEER SUPPORT

It still surprises me how many people I speak to who have never had a mentor or coach. They don't see the usefulness of it, and they tend to see it as a sign of weakness. Nothing could be further from the truth. It's a real sign of strength to show that we understand that learning is something that we continue to do, and that we should never feel that we have "cracked it".

Then, other people see it as a scarce resource and think we should only have one guide in the form of a coach or mentor, and they should be used sparingly. Instead, it is better to see guidance and support as thoroughly abundant. We should draw on those who are willing to coach us, to mentor us, and to give us peer support. We are greater when we are many, if we draw on the expertise around us, we find ways to achieve the miraculous.

The more senior we become in an organisation, the more important it is to ensure that we don't isolate ourselves. The solitary leader is a danger to herself and those in her team. Through a thirsty interest in others, our curiosity can build for us a lexicon of knowledge and a contact network of people that we can rely on for advice and support. Often this support is not in the form of direct advice. We may just be reaching out for someone to talk things through with, to have present with us to bear witness to what we say. This act of presence can give us the space to work things out for ourselves. For the person "sitting with" it is really important to realise when it is enough to just be there, and that no contribution is required.

RESILIENCE AND RESOURCEFULNESS

The "r" word has become so fashionable of late – resilience! It's a word with different meanings depending on the context. In the world of work, it is often used to mean – we will treat you really badly as an employee and occasionally we will run programmes for you to help you to find ways to cope with this. Resilience programmes are set up by organisations when they realise that they are struggling to retain staff and to manage the levels of morale. I am more interested in how the individual works with their own levels of resilience and resourcefulness. In the coaching space, there is often the opportunity for the coach to ask the client how they are coping with the challenges that they are facing.

A recipe of approaches that help build resilience would include:

- Time spent alone
- Learning meditation
- Reaching out to others for support
- Finding someone to mentor you that is not connected to your immediate work space
- Exercising
- Absorbing yourself in something that you enjoy e.g. music, film, reading

Taking any of these and making use of them, helps us to build the resilience we need, and give us perspective. When we are immersed in a challenging situation it can be really difficult to see it for what it is. Things become overwhelming really easily. Asking ourselves what this will be like in one year, five years and ten years can help us to see that things may not be as critical and all-encompassing at they seem at the time.

Chapter Four

CREATIVE

G ive me a pound for every time someone says to me "I'm not really creative" and as the saying goes, I would be a wealthy man! At some point in our journey through life, for many of us we find ourselves feeling inadequate when it comes to creativity, whether it's playing a musical instrument, painting, drawing or writing. Something shuts down in us – often because someone tells us that what we have produced is rubbish, or that we will never excel at what we are trying to learn. I had an art teacher at secondary school who told me that there was no point in choosing art as an option for the next school year because I was no good at it and couldn't draw.

Everyone has access to creative skills and abilities.

© Kate Taylor

This view shuts down access to a rich seam of skills, techniques and ideas. For the coach, it is really important to break down these barriers and find a way back into the creativity of the client. It is there, but it is closed down by the negative speak of "I'm not really creative" or "I can't draw" or any other combination of limiting belief statements. These statements need calling out – they limit the person who says them.

None of us are "not really creative". Everyone has access to creative skills and abilities. I'm not saying that we are all creative geniuses capable of achieving what da Vinci or Matisse did. We aren't all creative geniuses but we do have creative genius within us that can spark amazing ideas and solutions to seemingly intractable problems. There's a big difference between having genius and being a genius.

LEADERS INSPIRE WITH IDEAS

I have talked earlier in this book about the difference between leadership and leaders. We all have responsibility to lead, we all have the option to do so. When we feel empowered (or rather, when we take our own power), we open up the ability to lead, and to inspire others.

Creativity is so important in leading. We should learn as much as we can about creativity, so that we can apply techniques to the work and open up the potential in what we are doing. As a coach, working with leaders and those who realise the opportunities in leadership, it is vital to open up the client to the creative source within them. Michael Bungay Stanier, in his wonderful book "The Coaching Habit", describes a powerful technique to tap into this inner creativity. One of the key questions he identifies is "And what else?" This question moves the client beyond the first obvious answer. It pushed through, especially with repeated use, to further ideas, further solutions. The first solution is not always the best one. Skills of generating additional solutions, and of thinking laterally, can lead us into much more powerful ideas.

LEARNING FROM APPLYING CREATIVITY TO TEAM CONVERSATIONS

The traditional meeting approach of a group of people around a table, with a chair to lead the discussion, an agenda and a minute taker – all of this is designed beautifully to hinder creativity, to close down conversation. We need to jettison this approach wherever possible. No more hiding inside an agenda, closing down discussion and trust as we leap to first solutions, focused on the easy stuff, rather than the tricky things.

There are so many other ways to pursue meaningful conversation. Through coaching, we can work with the client to find more purposeful approaches to using conversation in the workplace. When a group of people come together, we need to ensure that we get the most out of everyone in the room. They all bring skills and expertise, the approach adopted needs to ensure that we are able to draw on all of that. Any group will have dominant members, introverts, passive members. The key thing is to find a way to draw out everyone's contribution. In Susan Cain's TED Talk and the accompanying book she emphasises the need to ensure that the introvert reflector is able to make their contribution to the work that we do. This doesn't tend to happen when the only technique used is the traditional meeting, which relies on people thinking on their feet, finding a way to be heard through the noise of opinions and jostling for airtime. Have you ever noticed how it is often the quiet members of the team who make the most insightful contribution. They may not talk a lot, but when they do it is really valuable. Adopting techniques, such as slowing down the conversation and asking people to jot down their thoughts in a quiet few moments before asking for contributions, makes sure that you get everyone involved.

Using other creative techniques, such as asking for drawings, diagrams or maps of what people are thinking, can also elicit ideas from people that draw on parts of their mind that they will not be used to using. These approaches can also be adopted in the coaching session. The traditional face to face conversation through questioning, can be broken down by shifting the rhythm, using post-its or getting the client to jot down their thoughts and map them out on paper.

To gain deeper insight into the client as a coach, we need to dig deeper, to tap into the resourcefulness that is at the heart of the client. Creative approaches may feel uncomfortable, but it is the discomfort that leads us to the insight that we are looking for. This is how we will make progress.

BRINGING OUT THE CREATIVITY IN PEOPLE

We sit down with our client, and we say to them, let's be creative. Let's paint or draw how we feel right now. This is a sure way to block the client. We can't just begin like that. The client will go into fight, freeze or flight mode. To bring out the creativity in the client, we need to be working at building trust, and easing them into the process, step by steady step.

In a coaching session, typically two hours long in my practice, there is a natural ark or rhythm to the session. The opening part of the session will be all about an update from the previous session and setting the agenda for the current session. Once the agenda is set – I usually restrict the client if possible to no more than three things to discuss, as that typically fits the time available and gives the necessary focus. We then decide where to begin, and go into diagnostic with the first issue. So far, this is all familiar territory for the typical coaching session. There then comes the point sometimes with a difficult topic / problem where the client is stuck. Sometimes this stuck-ness manifests in the coach too. Transference is a powerful effect – I can feel stuck too, and need to have enough self-awareness to recognise it and realise that it is the client's issue, not mine. I am picking up the feeling from them.

This can be where shifting the momentum in the session can be achieved by applying coaching techniques.

A simple way to do this can be by using a deck of suggestion cards. I have several of these. The first one I bought was the "Creative Whack Pack" by Roger von

Oech, which is full of superb techniques and disruptive ideas. Brian Eno created a creative ideas card pack with Peter Schmidt back in the 1970s that continues to evolve. It's called "Oblique Strategies" and can also be found online as a website. Each card creates a prompt. Eno has used this extensively as a music producer when working with artists to unblock them, and to generate something unpredictable. Either of these card packs can be really useful for bringing out creativity in the client. I also have a card pack created by Doug Shaw called "Stop Doing Dumb Things" which has really useful prompts in it too.

It is also worth exploring the willingness of the client to "draw" the problem. It is critical to emphasise that this is not about creating great art. We don't need to be able to draw proficiently in order to describe the problem in visuals. The trick is to find a way to get the client out of linear thinking, to come at the problem from a completely different perspective.

Maps can be a useful tool. We think of maps in a geographical sense – the ordnance survey map that shows us how to get from one place to another. But there are many applications of maps. For example, if the client is struggling with team dynamics and they think that this is created by a particularly difficult member of the team, using a map might help to see it differently. Getting the client to map out the team on a piece of paper, looking at how the relationships work within the team, can be a good first step to seeing new insights into what is going on. This may lead to new ideas about where the challenges are, rather than focusing on difficult relationships, we may end up looking at where the strengths are and seeing if it is possible to build from there. Model and reward good behaviour rather than spending all our energy trying to sort out bad behaviour. The map is a good way into this.

COACHING FOR CREATIVITY

Techniques that are drawn from the creative world can be so helpful in the coaching process. They help to open the client to possibility. The most common underlying theme in coaching is the need to work with the client to open them up to the opportunities that they have, to unpick the self-limiting beliefs that they have built up over the years. Embarking on a process that coaches specifically to enable a more creative outlook, to develop creative techniques, helps to address this fundamentally.

As I said at the beginning of this chapter, so many of us define ourselves as uncreative, as lacking in creative skills. This is at the heart of self-limiting beliefs. If we open ourselves to the possibility that anything can be attempted, that we can make poetry, we can make music, paint, draw, sculpt or carve – all of these are basic skills that we can learn. It's not about creating artistic genius. The important point is that all of these different techniques are creative languages that we can use to interpret the world around us. If we do this, we can then ensure that we are open to different ways of looking at things, we can be open to non-linear thinking, and we become open to the possibility of holding two opposing thoughts in the mind at the same time, accepting that both could be true.

Getting away from simple, linear and binary thinking enables the coaching process to develop an openness in the client. This generates the possibility that the world is complex, many things are possible, there is not one true and correct way with anything. And that is the path to deepened insight.

TAKING A CREATIVE PATH

It can seem uncomfortable, even awkward, when we first open the coaching session up with creative approaches. The important thing is for the coach to be open to the intuition. It's not about preparing for this in advance, having a set agenda that says "oh yes, I introduce drawing after 40 minutes or when the problem has been identified." That doesn't work because it feels staged. Instead, it's about being with the clients in deep listening, observing all the cues that are open to us, and listening for our own inner cues too. There will come a moment when our intuition (our gut instinct, if you like) will tell us that the linear path we are following is getting us nowhere and that we need to make a shift in thinking. This is the moment where it is time to jolt the momentum, to ask the client to dive into trying something different. Then we open up the idea of trying something creative.

It's often really helpful if we use this shift of gear to slow things down, hold the space and encourage intro-spection. In this mode, the client has time to think and time to absorb ideas. As the coach, it is important to be aware of the pace and the energy in the room, and adjust it in this way where it will really help.

So, we have a problem that we have been working with together for maybe 40 minutes and that feeling of stuckness emerges. That is the point where we say to the client, "I'll tell you what I feel stuck, do you? Shall we try something different? Let's unpack things a bit more, look at what we are dealing with here from a different perspective. Would you like to use a piece of paper and we can map out what this looks like?"

The coach needs to open this up with the intention of getting the client leading the interpretation, determining what things might look like and perhaps choosing the medium too. Then the coach can encourage the client to step back with them and look at the map together – see what they see that they may not have seen before. This is the way towards insight.

Chapter Five

PRODUCTIVE

Productivity is one of those recurring themes in coaching. And it seems like it's one of those issues that so clearly demonstrates the theory of entropy: every time we think we've cracked it, time passes and we slip back into old habits and inefficiency again. It's so frustrating. At least, it is until we realise that this is the state of things, and see each lapse as an opportunity to rebuild the processes again, open ourselves to experimentation and the scope to develop to the next level. Like acquiring belts in martial arts, each step requires us to unlearn some of what we learnt at the previous stage and to start again. In this chapter I am going to introduce a series of techniques that I share with my clients when we are looking at productivity. These techniques when built up over time, create the opportunity to develop a scaffolded approach that ensures increased productivity combined with growing self-reflection and the capacity to learn as we progress.

TOPIC DU JOUR

This is an idea I found in a fabulous book on journaling by Kathleen Adams. The book called "Journal to the Self" is packed full of useful exercises.

In this exercise, she suggested taking a different topic each day, and journaling on it. I've adapted this idea. For my Topic du Jour (TdJ for short) exercise, I produce a list of 31 different projects that I am working on at the moment. Then on each day of the month I take 10 minutes (measured with a timer) and write about that topic. It gives me the chance to really focus down and work out what I want to do with that topic in the short term. Each day of the month I pick off one of the 31 items. Then, every 3 months I review the list of topics to see whether any of the topics are out of time and need replacing.

It's as simple as that. It's a powerful exercise, helping to create a real focus and action around each project area.

This process is really powerful with a client in the coaching process. Often clients can find it difficult to see the wood for the trees. They may have a list of tasks that need doing (I will come back to the idea of a list in a moment), but they don't really have a clear grasp of the projects that they are working on, and the list they have will be a mix of simple tasks and complex projects. It's important to have a clear understanding of all of the projects that we are working on in the various aspects of our life. Spending a few minutes each day looking at one of these, can really help us to keep momentum, whilst not overwhelming ourselves with all of the projects at once.

The idea of a list is straightforward enough – most people have a list or lists. What bewilders me is how many people still keep this list in a book, hand-written – and have to keep writing it out again and again. Whilst repeatedly writing out the same stubborn task that we aren't getting to may help us to be aware of that, it's not the best use of time to keep writing things out. It's much more effective to keep an electronic list. This is the easiest thing to do. There are list apps on our phones and laptops. They can be really simple or more elaborate. What matters here is that we pick one that works for us, and then gets out of the way so that we can become productive. If it's too elaborate we will spend more time on list management rather than actually doing things.

It's easy to spend more time on 'list management'
rather than actually doing things.

© Kate Taylor

TEN MINUTES ON...

Coming back to the issue of the task that we keep putting off, I may be a coach but I am as prone to procrastination as anyone else. I used to watch tasks appearing on my list every day for ages, and I just wanted to get them done. This would be a mixture of fear and being overwhelmed. It might be something that I have built up so much in my head, that I don't want to get started because I may fail, or I don't want to start it because it's too big a task to do in one go.

When I have these feelings on some level I am right. It probably is too big to get done in one sitting, and it may be too difficult to unpack and get it right first time. This is where the "10 minutes on..." technique comes in.

This is a really simple technique. It needs a timer: it can be the timer in your phone; a manual timer from the kitchen; or an app. The main point here is that the time is ticking and you have to write. I use a silent timer with the time remaining clearly visible. For some people an actual ticking clock may be helpful, but some may find that too distracting.

Set the timer to 10 minutes and start writing or typing. With the topic or issue as the title, you just write whatever thoughts you have about the issue. Don't stop until the 10 minutes is up. When the 10 minutes is over, take a break. Then decide whether to return to the issue or leave it for another day. The key thing is that you have actually made a start on the issue. The freeze has been unfrozen!

It's just an easy way to trick yourself into getting started. If I am not getting straight back to the writing, I set myself a reminder in the future to come back to this and do another stint on it. That keeps the task unfrozen.

Often, the surprising thing is that whilst we have tricked ourselves into getting started, if we continue once the 10 minutes are completed, we will often make far more progress with this "difficult" task than we thought we would.

This technique can also be used for problem solving. You could see it as an opportunity to pursue inner dialogue, get thinking about the problem, and set out your thoughts on paper, but not for sharing. When I use the technique for problem solving I usually make sure that I take the last couple of minutes to draw together a summary of actions that I have decided to take as a result of the thinking that I have done on the topic. And again, I schedule to return to these notes on a specific day, when I can look at them fresh and see what I can take from the ideas in there.

DAILY QUESTIONS

This is a brilliant technique developed by Marshall Goldsmith, one of the world's leading coaches. Marshall has developed the idea of a daily log, a set of questions that we ask ourselves to ensure that we stay on track. We are looking for habits that we need to maintain or ones that we are trying to control, reduce or stop. Helpful questions would be things like:

- Did I exercise today?
- Did I meditate today?
- Did I show gratitude today?
- Did I work on my most important project today?

It can also be helpful to have quantifiable questions, so for example I ask myself every day how many emails are in my inbox. This helps me to see when the inbox is getting out of control. I also ask myself how many words I have written each day. Habits can become easier if they become part of this ritual. I also monitor my daily step count, the distance I walked in miles, as this is easy to capture from my smart phone.

I have 12 questions that I routinely ask each day, and they keep me on target, keep me focused on what I should be doing.

Going through the questions each day can help to keep a focus where it is needed. Marshall Goldsmith takes delight in telling everyone that he pays a woman to ring him everyday to ask him these questions and listen without judgement to the answers. Being compelled to answer the questions calls him to account. That's an amazingly courageous approach. I don't do that, but I do make sure that I complete the answers for every day (weekends I cut myself some slack, but still keep up with things like meditation practice) and review trends regularly to see whether there are things that I am not getting around to, and need to add in some corrective approach.

Encouraging the client to use this technique can introduce a helpful set of simple measures to look at habits that need focus. The accountability of writing them down means that we can look at long term trends. This helps to develop deeper insight into what is going on in the areas that we focus on. If we set a question that demands a number, and every day we have to keep putting a big fat zero next to it, we will end up doing something about it!

WEEKLY REVIEW

This process is taken from the book by David Allen called "Getting Things Done". If you haven't read this book, and are struggling with your productivity and overall effectiveness I strongly recommend that you read it. It's a classic, recently released as a second edition updated for the digital age! It breaks down the components of productivity into simple manageable processes. I probably recommend this book to at least 50% of my coaching clients.

For the weekly review, David Allen suggests that we complete this at a regular time each week. I always do mine on a Friday afternoon before I finish for the weekend. I have a series of prompts (adapted from David Allen) that I use to steer me through the process which typically takes up to half an hour depending on how out of control things have become through the week.

The important thing with this process is that it gets everything into a trusty system and out of the memory. There is no use trying to hold things in our head and remember all that we need to do. Our minds are not designed to do this. It just leads to stress and a chaotic approach if we do. So, the principle is that everything should be kept in a task system (it could be a simple as a list, or a more sophisticated task management app – I use "Remember the Milk". Knowing that everything is in the system and can be found enables us to get stuff done without worrying about what we have forgotten.

The checklist for the weekly review that I use covers the following:

Loose papers – I pull together anything that needs turning into an action, and scraps of paper, notes or ideas and turn them into clear actions.

Process notes – in my notes, which I keep in journal books, I make sure that I clearly identify any actions with an asterisk in a circle (*). During this stage of the weekly review I go through all my notes from the previous week capturing these tasks and adding them to my task list.

Review previous calendar data – I look back over the last couple of weeks to see if there is anything I need to do that I may not have added to my task list.

Review Upcoming Calendar – a two week forward look for anything that needs capturing in tasks, preparation for a meeting for example, travel arrangements etc.

Empty Your Head – this is a five minute space in which to check for anything that's been hanging around in my memory and needs capturing now. This could be something random, an errand that needs running, something I have been meaning to do for ages. The important thing is to capture it, decide what needs doing and when to do it.

Review Action Lists including Action Email folders – in

this section I am looking through the task lists, deciding the best time to do things, balancing out each day so that there is not too much to do. I am also looking through flagged emails to make sure that I have captured tasks from them.

Review Waiting-For List – including Pocket – this review process is focused on things that I am waiting for from others. A key tool for this is my email sent folder, which I review going back up to a month to look for emails that I haven't had a reply to and may need to send a reminder. I also use a simple app called Pocket to save things for reading later that I come across when web browsing. I review this to look for things that I need to make sure that I read.

Review Project (and Larger Outcome) Lists – a quick review of the key projects I am working on to see if there are any tasks that I need to do on them. Having a Topic du Jour list really helps with this – once a week I am skimming this project list to see if there are any actions I need to capture.

Review Any Relevant Checklists – I have various checklists that I use which I review at this point to make sure that I have captured absolutely everything.

Review Someday / Maybe List – some things that I would like to do are not time-specific. They sit in my system without a due date on them. They may not be urgent, and are ideas I would like to initiate at some point in the future. I do a quick review of this list each week to see if there are any things on it that I am now ready to do and should therefore move to a due date.

Be Creative & Courageous – and finally, I have a little time to think whether there is anything that I really want to step up to and do this week that will really move things forwards.

That's it! The Weekly Review. The version I have given here is very much based on David Allen's approach, with tweaks to fit the way that I work. The important thing is to be consistent as it is a space in the week to get things organised and gain perspective.

MORNING PRACTICE

So many writers recommend a form of morning practice. It is a key component for the practice of writers, artists and people in many walks of life. It's such a key building block at the beginning of the day. There is nothing worse than dashing into the day, racing to get out of the house on time, heading to work with no sense of focus or priorities, let alone understanding what the overall purpose of the day will be.

Over the years I have come across a lot of different approaches to the morning practice. Julia Cameron in her book "The Artist's Way" has a really useful exercise called Morning Pages, which she suggests should be hand written. You should write and keep writing until you have filled three pages, no editing, no pausing. Just write three pages of whatever comes into your head – it can be blah blah blah, it will often be the stuff we want to moan about. Whichever way you go into this, it's important to get it all out onto the page. Like a form of self-therapy, these words are not designed to be read back again. The exercise is a way to get all of the rubbish out of our heads so that we are ready for the day. I've done my own version of this exercise on and off for maybe 20 years now.

The best recent exponent of the morning practice as a whole that I have come across is Robin Sharma. He talks about the need for a 20/20/20 process. This requires us to spend the first hour of each day in three activities – exercise, reflection and growth. This is the morning mental and physical gym. We begin with physical exercise for 20 minutes, followed by 20 minutes of reflection time. This time can be taken with meditation or journaling, and then the third section of the hour is used for personal growth through reading or listening to audio materials. It's a really worthwhile discipline. I don't manage the degree of discipline and rigour that Robin Sharma describes in his book "The 5 am Club" but I do have quiet time to myself each morning where I can practice some of this and set myself up well for the day.

If we don't prepare ourselves for the day, get a small headstart and work out how we want the day to be, we will let the day take charge of us and spend it playing catch up.

A GRATITUDE DIARY

We don't see the world as it is, we see it according to the lens that we apply. That lens is affected by the mood we are in, and by what we are looking for. In the typical day we see only a small fraction of what appears before us. It has to be that way: even though our brains are incredibly sophisticated, they can't process everything that we see. We discriminate the images that appear, we decide what we will notice and then we apply another filter to make sense of it.

So, if we can use a simple technique that helps us to focus on things that improve our view of reality that must surely be a good thing. This is where the Gratitude Diary is valuable.

This exercise takes just a few minutes each day. Try it for 30 days and make sure you capture the results in a notebook. This makes it possible to review and check through the outputs. Doing it in the morning, perhaps as part of the Morning Practice, means that we set ourselves up well for the day.

There are five simple questions to respond to. Here they are:

1. What 3 great things did I do yesterday?
2. How could I have made yesterday better?
3. What am I grateful for?
4. What 3 actions would make today great?
5. What kind of person do I want to be today?

At the end of 30 days you will have 90 great things that you did, and at least 30 things that you are grateful for. It's a great way to avoid the victim thinking that happens when something goes wrong and we catch ourselves saying "uh oh, this is going to be a bad day". There is no such thing as a bad day. That is just a way that our mind constructs the reality that we are observing.

The final question of the five is really important to address as it sets the tone for the day. Do I want to be generous, patient, kind, compassionate, warm or friendly?

You can vary the questions to suit your needs. The important thing is that the emphasis of the questions is positive. Even if we are having challenging times, this exercise helps us to see the positive things around us, and gives us the resilience to push on through.

ONE HUNDRED QUESTIONS

I've been using this technique for about 10 years now. It's derived from an exercise in a book by Michael Gelb called "How to Think Like Leonardo da Vinci". This book is full of remarkable ideas and exercises. In the book, Gelb sets out the 7 different modes of thinking developed by da Vinci and describes how to apply each of them.

The 100 Question exercise is a fantastic exercise to focus in on the deeper issues that are bothering us at the moment.

Depending on the speed at which you type or write, allow about half an hour for this process. Without over-thinking it, and without breaking off, begin to write out 100 questions that address the things that are on your mind at the moment. Anything that comes up should be included, avoid the temptation to censor or edit as you go. At some point after you have got to 50, the exercise will probably start to annoy you, but keep going as this is probably the key point where the questions will go deeper.

After half an hour or so, you will have a list of 100

questions that address a wide range of issues in your life. When you have finished it, put it away for now.

I have a couple of additional approaches that I now apply to this list. After a few days, I return to the list and go through batches of 10 questions each day, looking for issues that I need to address and focus in on. I am looking for actions that I can pursue, or things that I need to do in response to that question. This makes sure that anything that appeared in the questions that needs attention isn't forgotten about. For example, one question might be asking why I haven't finished an important project – there's an obvious task in there that needs addressing!

After 10 days of doing this, having gone through the whole list – I go through the entire list and pull out 10 key questions that I think are the most important for me to address. Then, over another 10 days I take a question each day, and apply the "10 minutes on..." technique, so that I am expanding on that issue and coming up with some ideas to take forward.

This is an incredible approach to create real focus, and propel us forwards in key areas of our life. It takes effort, but the effort put in is more than rewarded by the outputs created.

Using 4D and 6D

Over the years I have adapted a number of techniques to help me to increase my productivity. The inspiration for these two techniques comes once again from the book "Getting Things Done" by David Allen.

In the book, Allen is really clear about how to clear our inbox of email so that it becomes a useful tool for our work, rather than a dumping ground or glorified filing cabinet. You may have heard of the concept of inbox to zero. This idea comes from this concept. We shouldn't leave things lying around in our inbox. That's the theory anyway. Of course, that works well when there is a steady flow of emails and we have ample time to deal with them. It all starts to unravel when we are busy for a day and don't have time to check our email, or the volume suddenly surges. Whatever the reason, at times like this we begin to slide into indecision. The priority becomes finding the key emails that we MUST reply to. Everything else starts to pile up in the inbox.

Then, it becomes really easy to just keep dipping in and out of our email, not really focusing on anything else.

4D - This is where the 4D technique comes in. It's really important not to keep looking at email every time something comes in. That just causes too much distraction. Find the optimal number of times for checking email – it may be twice a day, early in the day and towards the end.

Then, to optimise the time we commit – maybe half an hour – make sure that we are applying the following 4 options to what to do next:

- Do it (if it takes less than two minutes)
- Defer it to your task list
- Delegate it (if you have people to delegate to)
- Delete it

Being this ruthless about every email allows us to process large numbers of emails at speed. For the emails that need to be deferred, I have an action folder to send them to so that they don't stay around in my inbox.

It's easy to keep dipping in and out of your
e-mail and not focus on anything else.

© Kate Taylor

Nothing that is processed should stay in the inbox.

6D - That process will work for sorting the email inbox, but one thing it will also do is swell the task list with things that take longer than 2 minutes. Potentially we are now creating another space for procrastination. Sitting down at the start of the day with a huge task list can be daunting. Like the rabbit in the car headlights we can easily become frozen, unable to tackle the volume of stuff that faces us.

One key issue here is to ensure that we are being clear about what is important and what is urgent. That helps us to sort through and get to the things that we should be doing.

But there will always be tasks that are piling up and really need doing. This is where the 6D technique comes in. Sitting down with a pile of tasks on a list, we apply the 6D approach:

- Do it now if it's a short task
- Do 10 minutes on it to get it started (use the 10 minutes on technique)
- Defer it to the diary and book in time to do it
- Determine what it is (sometimes we put vague things on the task list and don't really know what we need to do)
- Delegate it
- Delete it (has the time passed? Is it still relevant?)

Using these 6 steps to look at each task can really help to tidy up the task list and get us moving again.

A PRODUCTIVITY SCAFFOLD

The approaches outlined in this chapter can give the client a set of techniques and exercises that will really shake up the way that they work. These are all approaches that I use regularly myself. They will need adapting to fit the style of the client. It's important not to suggest that they be adopted as they are. Productivity is a really personal thing.

A framework that underpins the way we work, which could comprise some of these techniques, will give the client real insight into maximising their effectiveness.

Chapter Six

MAVERICK

E very organisation needs a maverick or two to ensure that it doesn't become safe and "cosy" in its approach, because that leads to poor quality and bad outcomes. But the maverick can often feel like the odd one out, misunderstood or completely marginalised. If the maverick is lucky, they will find their way to a coach and begin the work that they need to do to develop inner strength to follow their path, and to find techniques that will help them to survive.

NOT FITTING IN

It is in the nature of human beings, as social animals, that we find our way to build tribes, to encourage belonging and conforming. This basic need is part of the way we build coherent communities. There is nothing wrong with listening to this urge to be a part of something. But for many of us, fitting in and following the norms doesn't always fulfil something deeper that drives who we are.

On a shallow level, we may hear advice that suggests we find an organisation or workplace where we can fit in, where the values and drivers align with our own. Whilst that is a good aspiration, and one that I addressed in my earlier book "Values Count", that isn't always possible. And we also need to recognise that sometimes we are there to achieve change. If we want to achieve our potential, and the things that matter to us are going to be actualised, we must find a way to push through the values and principles that are around us, and assert our own view of things.

This will lead to strong feelings of not fitting in. We will feel on the edge of the group. Margaret Wheatley describes this feeling beautifully when she names people in this situation as Edge Walkers. She also talks about the need for those who feel that they don't fit in, to connect together, to be an island of sanity in an otherwise insane world.

Not fitting in should not be the beginning of the steps towards changing ourselves so that we do fit in. It can feel like that, but this must be resisted. In a battle of wills, we can maintain who we are and what our values are, by quiet inner resistance at first. Little will be achieved in the early stages of this process of claiming our inner maverick, if we go into full-on protest mode. Doing that will put us too much out into the open, vulnerable to the rules of the tribe. This is a long journey that takes slow and steady steps to get there, a little at a time. Once we have seen that we do not fit in with the prevailing culture, we need to look at what that means for our everyday work. What is the driver for this? Is this mission critical? Can we find a way to hide in plain sight, whilst we figure out how to influence the changes that we want to see?

ROCKING THE BOAT

In the early 2000s I worked in a national agency within the NHS. I was lucky enough to have a great boss. This was Helen Bevan who had made her career from business process re-engineering, service redesign and a host of quality initiatives that followed these. This strand of thinking goes right back to the early quality work of W. Edwards Deming. Helen was an inspiration. She had an inner passion and drive, a deep-seated energy to change things for the better.

It was Helen who really made a major shift in my thinking when she pointed out that the change maker, the maverick, needs to be realistic about where they are with things. By all means take on the tradition of "this is the way we do things round here" and challenge it. Helen stressed that we can rock the boat to get things moving, but if we rock it too hard we will either fall out of our own accord, or we will be pushed out by the other passengers. It's a trick to learn to push with a clear understanding of what we are trying to achieve, whilst adhering to the key rules that matter to the organisation or community that we are working within. Some rules matter more than others. If we are going to break the rules to get where we need to go, we need to choose which ones we break. Don't rock the boat too hard and end up in the water, floundering and looking for another boat to clamber into.

How de we decide this? The coaching session is the perfect place to unpack these challenges, and to test out proposed actions in a safe space. The coach works with the client to open out the situation, look at it from various perspectives, encourage the client to think about how they are coming across to others in the organisation. If it's likely that others are seeing them as "a pain", an annoying distraction – it's important to look at this and decide what this is achieving. Who are the allies, and how does the client make sure that the boat is being rocked enough to be heard, and for them to share their ideas, but not so much that they either lose credibility or become seen as a troublemaker.

FRESH THINKING

Introducing fresh thinking into things will often be a risky thing to do. This disruption though, is at the heart of change. As I said at the start of this chapter, every organisation needs disruptors. We all need people who can give us constructive challenge and help us to move forwards and improve. The coaching process can be a way to introduce the client to new ways of thinking and to encourage the client to be curious and look for new ideas. Introducing ideas back into the team around them may need to be an incremental process – a little at a time, with the patience to realise that sometimes we have to keep coming back to something, drip feeding it in until it becomes more acceptable, something that is worth trying. I will return to this insight of Curiosity in a later chapter. For now, it's important to be aware of this need to get the client's curiosity awakened, alive to the possibilities that there are with everything that we see and do. Everything has an implicit question. When we approach the world around us with this questioning mind, we create the possibility that there is a better way of doing things. Approaching the world with this perspective, and being open to change, is what makes us become the Maverick.

Fresh thinking is at the heart of any vibrant organisation. Insightful coaching can support clients who are ready to go on that journey and keen to push at the status quo. Once equipped with the view that there is a better way to do things, that it is always worth looking at how something could be done better, that is when we are ready to push back at the way things are – and look for better ways to do them.

This is the point where the client needs most support, and needs to feel the safe space of the coaching session so that they can explore deep uncertainty and fear. This enables them to be their authentic self, look at how that will work in the outside world, and find support mechanisms to proceed.

LOOKING BEYOND

When we are at loggerheads with the organisation, and we feel that we can't win – it's key that we use the coaching session to open us out and take us beyond the here and now. In the moment, things can seem unbreakable, unsolvable. But that is when perspective becomes really important. The insightful coach can work with us to look out beyond the current situation. Skillful questions will help us to see that the world we are looking at is narrowed by our own view of it. Stepping up above and beyond the situation, we can look around for colleagues who feel like we do. If there is no-one in our organisation who agrees with our view, it's helpful to look beyond to other places. If our views and ideas have come from things that we have read, it's always worth considering writing to those whose views we are adapting. I've done this with many of the writers whose work has shaped my thinking. Not all of them reply, and not all will connect fully. Some do – and they really help to reassure us that it is not us, it's the challenge and resistance that we inevitably face as a push back. Connecting with Margaret Wheatley led me to a better understanding that there are fundamental, underlying ethics that determine the island of sanity. Out beyond that, where ethics are compromised, that is not a healthy world to live in. We need to push against this, protect our maverick spirit and find inner belief to continue to fight for what is right.

PROTECTING OURSELVES

I have made the role of the maverick seem pretty scary, perhaps. This is justifiable. In organisations where the challenge is often about survival, based on a capitalist model of constant growth and increasing profitability, and survival of the fittest, it will always be challenging to propose better ways of working. This is why we need to look for techniques to protect ourselves.

Coaches frequently work with people who are at the edge of things, challenged by what is going on around them, and feeling that they are often just a step away from rocking the boat too hard.

I've already talked about the importance of conforming to the rules that are sacrosanct − for example, adhering to the organisations basic paper trails so that we are beyond reproach.

The first step to protect ourselves is to get a clear understanding of our core values, so that we better understand why some things resonate with us, and others make us feel really uncomfortable. I have looked at this in detail in my book "Values Count".

Finding a group of people who we can rely on either one-to-one or as a coherent group, will give us the island of sanity that Margaret Wheatley talks about. These people may be in our organisation, but they are more likely to be further afield and will take work to discover.

Once we have a clear grasp of our values base and beliefs, we should spend time journaling about things. Write about what is going on around us, what we are comfortable with, and what we want to change. Capture what we can.

Using the coaching session as a space to explore what we are unhappy about, creates an opportunity to come up with a clear action plan to sort things out one way or another. Reading for inspiration will open our minds to ideas that may not otherwise have occurred to us.

Finally, sometimes it is important to know when to back down. Some battles cannot be won. There may be too much at stake for the organisation to let go of. An individual we are clashing with may not be prepared to let go. In either of these situations, we need to figure out whether we should let things go, or consider leaving. The wisdom to understand when we are engaged in a battle that we cannot win is priceless.

Principles can be really expensive, as a barrister who charges £1000 an hour will tell you.

I don't want to end this chapter on a negative note. Being a Maverick is a courageous thing to be. As I said at the start of this chapter, all organisations need Mavericks. Protecting ourselves and finding techniques to work through the organisation and get supporters for our ideas, even when they challenge the norms, can achieve remarkable things. We are in this world to make a difference, to leave things better than we found them. Sometimes we can't just quietly walk away.

INSIGHTS

A. TRANSITIONS

There are many types of transition in our lives. It could even be argued that life is one long transition as we age, mature and develop. But beyond the small incremental transitions that are happening day to day, there are major events that have a massive impact upon us. The most common one in coaching practice is redundancy or dismissal. Transition towards retirement is another process that lends itself to coaching interventions. Events outside the workplace like childbirth, divorce, moving house – all have an impact that needs to be processed and in some cases survived.

One of my favourite writers on the broad topic of Transitions is William Bridges. His books "Transitions: making sense of life's changes" and the organisationally focused 'Managing Transitions: making the most of change" are seminal works in this field. I strongly encourage you to read them. Bridges develops a model to handle change, developed from Jungian psychology and drawing heavily on Elizabeth Kubler-Ross's Five Stages of Grief model, he stresses the importance of the emotional context of change. This is unusual in change theory, where the prevailing paradigm is to look at rational and logical models of change and determine how to proceed. Emotion isn't logical – it needs time and space to do its work. Coaching can bring us into a deeper insight about the transitions that happen in life.

PEARL IN THE OYSTER

Life is suffering. It is also a series of opposites, concepts that co-exist because they are the opposite of each other. You can't have happiness without sadness, darkness without light, fear without love, joy without pain. When we pass through a period of transition, we experience all of these conflicting feelings day by day. We want it all to stop. We want a return to some certainty.

Life is ticking along just great, the job is fun and we feel comfortable. We are paid well and we enjoy what we do. Then, out of nowhere the news comes that the organisation is going to have to make 30% of the staff redundant. We didn't ask for this, we want the world to go back to how it was.

The series of opposites co-exist. Within happiness there is sadness. One can't exist without the presence of its opposite. It is the little piece of grit within the oyster's shell that causes the irritant that over time becomes a beautiful pearl. It is the things that go wrong, the unravelling that happens every so often, that brings the pain of transition – and that will lead in time to something magical, to a pearl being created.

It is difficult to see the positive when we are in the midst of the storm, and everything is plunged into uncertainty. Insightful coaching encourages the client to let go, to be in the moment. We need to be clear about the things that are out of control – and let go. Somewhere in all of the chaos, there will be something that we can control. That is what we should focus on. This may be something external – if so, grab hold of that. Typically, everything outside of us is out of our control. The only thing that we can control is our thoughts. That is when it is time to journal – write down what we are thinking, and notice what is going on. Find a positive way to look at things. For example, I can't change what is happening and I can't influence the outcome, but I can change how I react to it. I am going to go into this situation each day and be as positive as I possibly can be.

THE JOB CHANGES WHETHER WE LIKE IT OR NOT

The changes that happen around us in work are so often out of our control. They happen regardless of what we think about it. Coaching is one way to be clear about what we have control of. Getting frustrated and stressed about things that aren't under our control is futile.

A change of boss, change of job duties, sideways move, someone being promoted when it should have been me; these are all things that we don't have control of.

The coaching session is a place to come to understand this, and to then shift our mind-set so that we understand that it is our mind that we can change, that we can control. Any of these situations become opportunities for us to respond to. Instead of adopting a victim stance and railing against the situation, we look at it calmly and figure out what we can do about it. For example, if we are due to be made redundant, this is an opportunity to sit down with our coach and look at our options. Firstly, what is in our control? There may be some obvious choices that we can make – and then there may be choices that are less obvious because they are hidden from us by false assumptions. Thinking outside of the obvious solutions can get us to somewhere completely different and really exciting. The work that we do and are paid for by our employer, may be something that they don't want in its current form anymore. Do they want to buy it from us in another way, such as freelance? Does anyone else want to buy it from us? Can we adapt what we do so that it is of interest, transferable skills? Can we change the model completely to get a different solution? If we adopt some of the creative techniques mentioned in the earlier chapter, does this give us more insight into the problem?

LIFE CHANGES WHETHER WE LIKE IT OR NOT

The same principles that I have just described for the workplace apply to other aspects of our life too. A relationship breakdown, challenges of parenting or even just the basic stress caused by moving house – all of these will happen when they do. We can't stop them from happening. Each life event helps to shape us, and if we are reflecting and observing, learning from each event – we will become wiser as we age.

It's the working model of the Serenity Prayer:

*Grant to us the **serenity** of mind*
  to accept that which cannot be changed;
  courage to change that which can be changed,
  and wisdom to know the one from the other.

And yet this simple common sense so often eludes us. Insightful coaching picks up these issues and addresses them in the coaching session. Even when the coach is a workplace or leadership coach, everything is part of the story. Life events need to be part of the conversation too. A holistic approach to coaching realises that all aspects of our lives interact, and we can't ignore anything.

WHEN NO DECISION IS A GOOD DECISION

At times when we are under great stress, we can often feel that we need to unlock the huge amount of pressure by making a decision, any decision. This is a risky time for the client. If it is a decision between staying in a job or leaving, applying for a job or sitting tight – it can seem like a simple binary decision. But there is always a third option – to not make a decision either way just yet.

Sometimes, no decision is a great choice.

© *Kate Taylor*

Sometimes no decision is a great choice. There is a time when it is right to move forwards one way or another. Knowing when that situation is with us, is often something that we instinctively are aware of, but we suppress those feelings, because we think that logic should prevail. We should write out a list of pros and cons, then just make our minds up.

Staying in the discomfort of the uncertainty can feel excruciating, but it can lead to a better decision when it is time to decide.

An insightful coach can create the space and the challenge to make sure that the client doesn't jump to a conclusion too soon.

Often there is no simple answer to making a difficult decision.

© *Kate Taylor*

STAGES OF LIFE CRISIS

Sometimes the feeling of transition can be much more difficult to define. It's not that there is an external event happening that is influencing how we feel. It's something we can't quite describe. We have all heard of the mid-life crisis. I'm not convinced that this phenomenon is that linear, or that it is a one-time event. These phases of change come over us at regular intervals through our life as we come to terms with shifting perspectives on our life. They can often be the way that we view ambition, parenting, mortality, illness. It's not the external event or the passing of time that is the issue, it's the way our thoughts and feelings are shifting in the light of the age that we have become.

We know that the dark night of the soul, or the powerful feelings of unease that overwhelm us, are going to happen whether we resist them or not. The coach can help the client to see that things are just as they are, it is normal and part of who we are.

INDIVIDUATION

Carl Jung identified a really fascinating concept called Individuation. He argues that we come into this life as a fully formed being. As we go through childhood and into adult life, we fragment. This is due in part to our desire to please. We behave differently in different groups as we try to fit in. Our sense of self becomes fragmented into a series of characters that we play. We will be different when with our family to how we are when with friends, and different again when with work colleagues.

Beneath all of this there is a driving force that pushes us to actualise. The process of individuation takes the fragmented self, and pulls it into a fully coherent sense of who we are. We stop being different, we integrate the different parts of ourselves into our understanding of who we are. This individuation process drives these life stages, and causes us to make decisions about our lives that may not appear rational, but makes absolute sense to our concept of self.

It's only a theory but it's a compelling one. In coaching clients I often draw upon it to help them to understand that a decision they are attracted to might not make sense on a logical basis. For example, they may be less wealthy, have to commute further or want to change to a completely different career. But the driver behind it, which makes the choice they want to make so compelling, is the individuation process. They are moving forward to connect the fragments of self into a more coherent whole. With that lens, their decisions make absolute sense.

B. CURIOSITY

THE LIBRARY TRUNK

I grew up in a small village in the middle of England, about as far from the sea as you could possibly get. There were only 650 people living in the village. It had its own school – but there were only 21 pupils. My year was a big year – there were 4 of us!

Because the school was so small, it relied on resources being brought out from the nearest town. One of these was the library trunk. It looked like the kind of trunk that a world explorer would use, filled with all of their belongings. It was brown, sturdy and big enough for the smaller children to fit into if it hadn't been full of books.

Each month the trunk arrived, filled with a new stack of books. I looked forward to that day with so much excitement. I knew that I had a month in which to pick the best books, and get them read before the trunk was swapped again. The way the books arrived, the fantastic choice of books (thanks to the librarian who we never met) and the time limit all generated an enormous sense of curiosity in me. This is where my obsession with reading grew from.

As a coach, I think it is really important to encourage reading as a habit, and more importantly an obsession with curiosity. Seeing the world around as infinitely interesting, seeing everyone we meet as a source of fascinating stories.

I mentioned in the chapter on creativity, that it is quite common for clients to say that they "aren't really creative". The same can apply to reading. "I don't really get time to read books. Can't remember the last time I read anything." That's not true of course – we are all reading things every day, absorbing ideas from the laptop screen, the smart phone, the magazine, the newspaper. All around us there are words. We are constantly reading. It's just that for many of us, we don't actually sit down and read a book anymore. If I can encourage a few people to read a book, it feels like I've made a difference.

Making books, and the knowledge that they hold, feel as exciting as the library trunk of my childhood, is a worthy challenge for the coaching process. It's not just books, it's the whole process of learning, of curiosity and of being reflective about how we do things.

It's important to encourage
reading as a habit.

© Kate Taylor

LIFE AS A SAND PIT

Going back to that primary school class room, for the first few years of schooling, there was a sand pit, which was an essential part of each day. There were no standard attainment tests then and play was seen as a vital part of child development. I don't think I was alone in really looking forward to the time devoted to playing with the sand pit. It was a large tank with sand in it and a mix of toys – sometimes we got to add water as well, which took things to a whole new level. This was where I learnt to use my imagination and to be sociable too. I learnt to take turns, and to develop games where others took part.

I'm only half joking when I say that it is a shame that we don't have adult versions of the sand pit available to encourage play and curiosity. Adult life is so serious!

The coaching session can be a very serious space too. The challenges brought to coaching are often the cause of a lot of emotion, much of it negative. Play and curiosity can be an opportunity to transform this into a more positive perspective.

Insight coaching can draw on the techniques of play to open up a space of possibility, using curiosity as a way into a difficult problem. For example, if a client brings a problem with their relationship with the boss to a session. It can be a very heavy and challenging conversation. Or, it can be taken into a different space. Using curiosity and play, we can experiment with the interactions that haven't been working. Ask the client to look at examples of conversations that didn't work well – be curious about what is happening, and ask the client to imagine other ways this could have gone. Don't stop at the first one, ask for a handful of scenarios. Play with this – treat it like a drama workshop where we are creating scenes to try out. Then look at what the client could do to shift the conversations into this different space.

We see the reality that reflects what is in our mind. The world outside is a mirror of our inner world. If we keep seeing the relationship with our boss as a problem, it will build and become self-affirming. Imagining it in a different way is the first step to changing our inner perceptions of what is going on.

ANSWERS IN MY POCKET

It's not new to point out that the smart phone in our pocket makes the library trunk of my childhood seem like a matchbox of knowledge. The internet creates opportunities to be endlessly curious. I can find the answer to any question I pose. With some skills focused on checking the legitimacy of the answers I find, I can develop my curiosity and see each day as an exciting new learning experience. This is all part of the building blocks that we should encourage our clients to create. The client of insight coaching, can then go into the world with a curious mind, open to possibility and alert to the wealth of opportunities that are all around them.

TWO HOURS OF DISCOVERY

With a mind open to curiosity, the two hour coaching session becomes a panoply of discovery. Beginning with the issues that the client presents, the coach has the opportunity to hold the space as the client unpacks each issue and looks for insight, exploring possible solutions. The coach creates an atmosphere of open curiosity, expansive and broad. Opening the client to all of the possibilities that exist within the problem that is presented. Role modelling a curious mind, helps the client to see what they can do if they pull back, investigate and adopt the insight of some searching for ideas. It's an exciting process. Once the client takes the leap, they can become really excited by the journey they find themselves on. A problem which can begin as a really heavy, frustrating issue – can be opened out into a playful space where there are so many options open to the client, where they sense a growing feeling of control.

The power of curiosity is mind-blowing. Forget the catch-phrase that 'curiosity killed the cat'. That's nonsense! Through persistent curiosity we can get to more skilful solutions, and also find a much more exciting way to look at the world.

BEGIN WITHIN

The coaching session begins with the challenges brought by the client. It's not the coach's agenda. This can make the work of the coach a scary prospect. We enter the coaching session with no specific agenda, with no pre-prepared ideas (here's one I made earlier!), and feel often somewhat out of control. And that's good. That's how it is supposed to feel.

The client brings one, two or three problems or issues that they want to work through. It is really important that coach doesn't look at the coaching process as an opportunity to show how good a coach they are. The session is all about the client, not the coach. Techniques and tools are useful for the coach, but ultimately they are props that can hinder as much as they can help. The basic underlying principle of Insight Coach is a fundamental belief that the resourcefulness and the insight sits within the client. They have all that they need to resolve the problem that they face. The coach needs to work hard on getting their ego out of the way, sitting back and creating the space for the ever-resourceful client to use their curiosity to get where they need to.

Solutions begin within. The answer that we come up with for ourselves is always so much more powerful than one that is given to us. We are so much more likely to work with our own solutions. The coaching space is the place where we are given the luxury of a sand pit to explore until we come up with the solution.

© Kate Taylor

C. PURPOSE

THE ACORN THEORY

In his 1996 book "The Soul's Code", James Hillman set out his Acorn Theory. Hillman trained with Carl Jung in Zurich and went on to set up the Archetypal School of Psychology. The Acorn Theory is Hillman's take on an ancient idea, the idea of the driving force within us to become who we are destined to be. In the time of Plato this was known as the daimon. Philip Pullman uses the concept in the "His Dark Materials" trilogy.

Hillman says that we have an image that is the essence of our life. This is our destiny in the same way that the acorn is destined to become an oak tree. The oak tree-ness of the acorn is there in its seed. You could draw analogies to DNA and other aspects of humanity with this.

For the process of insight coaching, the key thing is

for the coach to be aware that they are in a dance with the client, looking for the destiny. It's in there somewhere: through the dialogue of the coaching session there is the opportunity to find the client's deeper purpose.

SENSE FROM NONSENSE

The client will bring their problems and challenges to the coaching session. Sometimes they will be bewildered by everything that they are confronting. In the moment, it is difficult to see the larger map, the overall picture that is being portrayed. Everything can seem like a random set of events, a state of nonsense.

But there is meaning in everything that happens to us. Every event has its cause, its purpose and its relevance. The coach works with the client to bring sense to everything.

We will not make sense of things if we look at them in a linear way. Stepping back, pulling apart all of the events and situations surrounding a problem, we may see patterns and links.

At this stage in understanding, the key thing is to support the client's outlook, reach for optimism – a realisation that everything does happen for a reason even if it's not obvious. Step by step we can help the client to move forwards, find a path that works for them.

UNFREEZING

Placing the overlay of purpose onto the coaching session, the coach can then see the process of insight coaching as being about unfreezing the client. We help the client to lift their awareness beyond the day to day, stuck as they often are in the challenges of the job. Each of these small challenges has buried within in, the prospect of digging deeper into the raw materials of realisations. With patience, the client can be brought to awareness that brings the real "aha" moments for them and creates the transformation that we want coaching to make happen.

When the "aha" moment happens, this is when the client begins to unfreeze, to make the giant leap forwards. They will reach other stages of confusion of course, this isn't a one-time solution. It's an ongoing process of discovery, progress, confusion and further discovery.

VALUES AS COMPASS

My previous book on values based working looking extensively at the inner work we must do to understand the core values that drive us. When we are clearly aware of our core values, we can use these as the compass to guide us to our core purpose. Our purpose defines the spaces where we will be at ease and growing, and steers us away from work and other spaces that are toxic for us, that sap our energy and demoralise us.

We use the compass to steer our course.

A VOCATION

This core purpose then is what we mean by vocation. In simple everyday terms we use the word 'vocation' to describe someone who has a clear professional path like being a doctor, an accountant, a priest.

One dictionary definition of the word is 'calling', which gives us a richer sense of how vocation can reflect the acorn theory. The drive within us to be fulfilled in what we do. That sense of vocation doesn't have to fit neatly into a recognised career path, a specific job. Instead, it becomes about making choices that fit with our inner purpose, choosing to be where we can make a difference in a way that is meaningful for us.

LIGHTS ON

And then the lights come on. For the client at this point, there is an awareness that they are now on a path that feels right. There is an illumination that helps to take them forwards. Purpose, when defined and used as the lens to make sense of the world, helps us to understand the world as we see it.

D. REALITY

As we come towards the end of the book, we come face to face with reality. It's important when we coach a client that we are constantly aware of the reality that we are within. What's happening for the client? How are they interpreting what they are bringing to the session? Remember always, that in the coaching conversation we are only hearing one version of reality. We only have the senses of the client to rely on.

We can check for clues within the story that the client is telling us, and we may then become aware of things that aren't obvious to the client.

We also need to look at the version of reality that the client is using. Are they working with something that serves them, or is their sense of reality working against them?

THE GAP BETWEEN STIMULUS AND RESPONSE

For example, I often find in the coaching process that the client has a mis-perception of the way that process works. They may find themselves in a situation of conflict with a colleague or family member. They will say, "He presses my buttons. I just know that when he behaves in a certain way he will make me angry". Or they will say the magic words, "It's just how I am."

These phrases contain some important flags. When the client says someone else is making them feel an emotion, that needs calling out. So does the expression "that's how I am".

Other people don't make us feel things. If we think that way, we are missing out an important step in the process. There are three steps: first there is the stimulus; then we have a choice; then we respond. The choice that we make in the gap, either happens spontaneously and without thought, or we can pause and think about the best way to respond. Many people don't notice this middle step. That's why they blame other people for their feelings.

When we say that we are a particular way, that's just not true. We have freedom to make choices. If we say that we get angry when certain things happen – that's just how I am – we are denying ourselves the free will to behave differently. We can change ingrained habits.

Pointing out to clients this step of choice is hugely empowering. It creates a space for the client to use a wiser decision to move forwards.

WE CONSTRUCT OUR REALITY

This understanding can be taken even further than this. All of our reality is invented in our minds. There is no objective reality. Take the situation that you are sitting in as you read this book. Around you there will be many objects, colours, textures and so on. Your mind is choosing what it sees. Many things in the space around you are not being noticed by your mind. You will also be choosing how deep to go with your version of reality, how much detail are you noticing.

This is not just a set of semantic games. It's an important level of understanding. Once we realise that we construct our reality in this way, this gives us the insight to realise that we are free to construct all aspects of reality in a way that serves us better.

When awful things happen – which they will do – we can choose to react as a victim, feel the pain and head on into a fight, flight, freeze reaction. Does that serve us in the long run?

Or we can slow it down, look at what is going on, and use coaching as a process that helps us to re-frame the situation. There will be another way to look at and shape reality so that we are able to move forward in a more constructive way.

So much is in our control if we realise that it is often not what is happening that is the issue, but how we react to it.

SOMETIMES IT HURTS

Bad things happen. This is inevitable. Suffering in life will happen to us from time to time. No-one goes through life without experiencing the loss of a parent, a loved one, relationships breaking down, becoming estranged from a friend, losing a job, being bullied in the workplace.

Sometimes life hurts. Accepting that is a key part of insight. Fighting against it is futile. How we live our life will enable us to handle whatever is thrown at us.

Understanding our values, and living by them so that we are congruent in all that we do, is a good start. A lifetime's teaching suggests that the route to happiness is in showing compassion for others.

These insights, when the client realises them in the coaching space, can bring the realisation that there are ways to tackle life in flow, rather than in resistance.

Sometimes we have to realise that we are not in control of other people or events.

© Kate Taylor

LET IT BE

I know it's the title of a song and album by The Beat-les. I should do as I've lived in Liverpool for 40 years now. The message in the phrase – sometimes we can't change things, there is no easy answer to the intractable problem. Things happen that are out of our control, we will be trapped by circumstances. Let it be. I talked earlier in the book about sometimes needing to wait to make a decision. That's true. Sometimes, it's also about realising that we are not in control of others or of events. We need to let it be. The transformation that we need to make is not in the outside world, it's in our minds. Thinking it differently, feeling it differently – these are the steps to take to reveal insight. All becomes clearer when we let go and let be.

BEYOND MEANING

As the reader of this book, you are probably wondering why we are heading into the meta-physical. Don't worry. As we head into a sense of deeper reality through insight coaching, we go beyond meaning.

What do I mean by this?

There are so many parts of coaching that are about dialogue, about questions and answers. When that works it's a fantastic process.

Sometimes the problem is beyond words, beyond explaining.

When this happens, it's holding the space together, realising that something has just made sense even though the sense of it is impossible to put into words. The holding of a silence with the client can be a powerful technique to allow sense and a shift to gradually emerge. That deeper insight beyond meaning is the work, done together, that leads the client to resolve.

CLOSING

So many techniques, so much advice across the chapters of this book. Here we are then, nearing the end of the book. Throughout this book I have set out to show you how transformational coaching can be, and to demonstrate to you the profound impact of coaching. There are many books out there about coaching, which describe techniques, models and approaches. In this book, I wanted to go deeper, and thereby show you that the influences I have cited in the book – from Jung to Hillman, Allen to Covey, Wheatley to Bridges – all combine to support my practice as a coach.

I have found over the years, working with clients from many backgrounds, that it is not just the practical conversations that matter. The really profound work in coaching comes when the coach gets out of the way, provides provocation and re-frames so that the client can realise a greater insight through the power of conversation.

A trusting conversation has power beyond the mere words that are spoken. When we experience this, we are transformed beyond who we are to who we become. That is a precious gift. I owe a huge debt to the coaches who have worked with me over the years, and to the clients who I have worked with in turn. Each of them, in their own sharing of the journey we are on, has brought a fragment of what I have ended up with in this book.

With my deepest gratitude to them all.

Stuart Eglin

FURTHER READING

These are some of the books that influenced the ideas I set out in this book. I frequently recommend them to clients to read between coaching sessions as a way to go deeper on a topic.

David Allen – Getting Things Done (Piatkus, 2015)

William Bridges – Managing Transitions (Nicholas Brealey, 2003)

William Bridges – Transitions (Da Capo, 2004)

Michael Bungay Stanier – The Coaching Habit (Box of Crayons Press, 2016)

Michael Bungay Stanier - The Advice Trap (Box of Crayons Press, 2020)

Stephen Covey – The Seven Habits of Highly Effective People (Free Press, 1989)

Mihaly Csikszentmihalyi - Flow (Rider, 1992)

Stuart Eglin – Values Count (BlueWater Books, 2017)

James Hillman – The Soul's Code (Bantam,1996)

Carl Jung – The Archetypes and the Collective Unconscious (Routledge, 1991)

Cal Newport - Deep Work (Piatkus, 2016)

Tom Peters - The Brand You (article in Fast Company can be found here on the internet https://www.fastcompany.com/28905/brand-called-you)

Alexander Osterwalder & Yves Pigneur - Business Model Generation (John Wiley & Sons, 2010)

Daryl Sharp – Who am I really? Personality, Soul, and Individuation (Inner City, 1995)

Daryl Sharp – Personality Types: Jung's Model of Typology (Inner City, 1987)

Margaret Wheatley & Deborah Frieze – Walk Out Walk On (Berrett Koehler, 2011)

Margaret Wheatley – Who Do We Choose to Be (Berrett Koehler, 2017)

WITH THANKS

Books don't get written without a lot of support from those around us. I would really like to thank June Eglin-Lowe for her unbounded patience and belief in the possibility that I would get to the end of this project. June has also become a part of the team supporting the writing of this book, along with Kate Taylor whose illustrations brought so much to the book, and gave fantastically irreverent observations to my ideas. Amanda Craig completed the team with her editing skills which have really helped to give the manuscript shape.

My ideas are the better for all of the people whose work I have read in books, on blogs and in podcasts. Some of them are referenced in the further reading section, but there are so many more whose work really inspired me.

Every coaching client I have worked with over the years, and there have been over one hundred, has given me something from the work we did together. Sometimes it has been an idea to help them get unstuck, sometimes it was a new technique worked through together, and sometimes it was just the reminder of the privilege of working with clients on the fragment of their life journey that they share with me.

I also owe a lot to those who have supervised my coaching practice - Su Fowler-Johnson and Roger Williams. Their input to the way I work has shaped my practice over the years.

It doesn't make sense to coach if you don't have a coach yourself. Over the years I have worked with six coaches, each bringing their own richness of skills and experience to guide me on my path. Thanks must go to Tony Betts, Ben Shoshan, Amanda Super, Val Michej, Su Fowler-Johnson and Ian Pettigrew for having the patience and insight to work with me and tease out what you find here.

And finally, thank you to you for reading this book. Do let me know if you find material in it which is useful to you. You can contact me at:

stuart.eglin@gmail.com

ABOUT THE AUTHOR

Stuart Eglin is: a writer; a leadership coach; a freelance consultant; a social entrepreneur and creativity expert.

Stuart is a Master Practitioner Coach, accredited by the European Mentoring and Coaching Council. He works part-time in the NHS in England where he leads work on strategic development of Research & Development for the North West region.

He has a PhD in organisational change from Manchester Business School where he studied the psychological aspects of change within organisations in the NHS, focusing particularly on applications of Jungian and Archetypal Psychology.

Feel free to get in touch on stuart.eglin@gmail.com

Stuart's blog can be found here:

www.stuarteglin.com/blog